# MACHINE LEARNING

# THE ULTIMATE GUIDE FOR THE

# ABSOLUTE BEGINNER

**An Easy Step by Step Deep Dive into Big Data Programming
with Python and C++**

# TABLE OF CONTENTS

# INTRODUCTION

Machine learning is currently empowering computers to handle jobs that have, until now, been completed by individuals.

To translating speech from automobiles, machine learning is forcing an explosion at the capacities of intelligence to make sense of this unpredictable and messy world that is real.

But just what is making the machine learning affluent on the computer?

Machine learning is the process of feeding info about the best way to create predictions instructing a computer system.

The difference from computer applications is that a programmer has not written code which instructs the machine to tell the difference between the apple cider and the banana.

Machine learning is the analytic model. It's a branch of artificial intelligence based on the concept that systems identify patterns that may learn from data and make decisions.

Machine learning is a tool for turning data into knowledge. There has been an explosion of information. This mass of information is futile unless we locate the patterns and examine it. Machine learning methods are utilized to find the valuable patterns in data that we would struggle to detect. Knowledge about an issue and the routines may be used to execute all sorts of decision making and to forecast future events.

# CHAPTER 1
# WHAT IS MACHINE LEARNING

Machine learning is what computers do, which comes naturally to people: learn from experience. Machine learning algorithms use computational procedures to "find out" information straight from the material without relying upon a predetermined equation for a model. Their functionality adaptively improves as the number of samples for learning rises out there. Education is a kind of machine learning.

Machine learning is a program of artificial intelligence (AI) that supplies systems the capability to learn and improve in expertise without being explicitly programmed automatically.

The method of learning starts with information or observations, such as immediate experience examples, or education, to make better choices in the future we supply and to search for patterns in data. The intention is to permit the computers to adapt actions and to understand them without human intervention.

Machine learning is used by many to improve advance living. It includes procedures that are professional but also industrial. However, what is machine learning? It's a subset of artificial intelligence, which concentrates on using statistical approaches to find out from databases to construct computer systems. Machine learning is used in businesses and disciplines like medical investigation, picture processing, prediction, classification, learning institution, regression, etc.

Machine Learning is one of the most influential technologies in the world today. We are far from viewing its entire potential. There is no doubt; it is going to continue to be creating headlines for the future. The following guide is designed as an introduction with no too large level, covering all of the basic ideas.

The majority of us are unaware that we interact with Machine Learning every moment. Each time we Google something, hear a tune, or even have a picture, Machine Learning is getting a part of the motor behind it, always learning and progressing from each interaction. It is also behind improvements that are world-changing like self-driving cars, producing new medications, and discovering cancer.

The rationale Machine Learning is fascinating is that it is a step away from our previous rule-based methods of:

If (x = y): do z

Software technology combined human-created principles with information to make answers. Machine learning utilizes replies and data to discover the principles.

# Traditional Coding vs. Machine Learning

Machines need to learn the principles regulating a happening. They work according to their role and by trying different rules.

There are kinds of Machine Learning unsupervised, semi-supervised, and reinforcement learning. Every type of Machine Learning has diverse perspectives, but all of them follow theory and the same process. This explanation covers the Machine Leaning theory that is overall and focuses on every strategy.

## Terminology

Dataset essential to solving the issue

Model: The rendering (internal version) of a happening a Machine Learning algorithm has discovered. This is learned by it from the information. The release is after instruction, an algorithm, the outcome you receive. A decision tree algorithm could be trained and generate a decision tree design.

## Procedure

Data Collection: Collect the information the algorithm will learn from.

Information Preparation: plan the information format, making the reduction, and extracting attributes

Assessment

Tuning

# Origins

Ada Lovelace, one of the creators, possibly, and of calculating the computer programmer. It could be clarified with mathematics.

This meant a formula could be made to derive the connection. Ada Lovelace understood that machines possess the capability to comprehend the world with no need for aid.

These ideas are crucial, even after around 200 decades in Machine Learning. Machine Learning attempts to obtain the patterns and relationships hidden within the initial info.

# Probability Theory

Probability is an orderly view. According to Thomas Bayes, it is the inference from information and the revision of this view in the light of pertinent new information.

Thomas Bayes, a mathematician, gave this theory.

We reside in a probabilistic world. Everything that occurs has uncertainty. The Bayesian interpretation of probability is that which Machine Learning relies upon. Bayesian probability means measuring the difficulty of the event, we think.

As a result of this, we must base our probabilities information available about an event, instead of counting the number of trials. When calling soccer games, rather than counting the number of occasions Manchester United has won from Liverpool, a Bayesian strategy would utilize details like the form beginning and putting team.

The advantage of taking this strategy is that probabilities can be assigned to occasions, as the procedure is based on rationale and features.

## Machine Learning Approaches

There are types of machine Learning grouped into the areas. Unsupervised and supervised are the most utilized approaches. Reinforcement Learning and semi-supervised are more complicated and newer but have shown remarkable results.

There are plenty of strategies and algorithms to match each issue of quirks. More fashions of AI and Machine Learning will remain being released that best-fit problems that are distinct.

- Supervised Learning

- Unsupervised Learning

- Semi-supervised Learning

- Reinforcement Learning

## Supervised Learning

In supervised learning, the Objective is to understand the mapping (the principles) between a pair of inputs and outputs.

The inputs could make the weather prediction. And the outputs are the traffic to the shore. Supervised learning's objective is to find out the mapping which describes the number of beach visitors and also the connection between temperatures.

Example labeled information is supplied of the output signal and input Pairs throughout the learning procedure to instruct the version it ought to act 'supervised' learning. For the shore example, inputs can be fed from prediction temperature as well as the Machine learning algorithm will lead to a forecast.

Being able to adapt to new inputs and create predictions is the generalization component of machine learning. We would like to optimize generalization. Therefore, the aerodynamic model defines the actual 'overall' connection. We induce over-fitting into the cases if the version is over-trained, and the release would not be able to accommodate new inputs.

A negative effect of being conscious in learning is the prejudice. The version may be copying what has been revealed. Therefore, it is essential to show it dependable, illustrations that are unbiased. Before it accomplishes, supervised learning needs a whole lot of information. Obtaining labeled data is of using supervised learning, the most expensive and toughest portion.

The output from a Machine Learning version could be a class in the restricted set, e.g. [low, medium, large] to the amount of traffic to the shore:

Input [temperature=20] -> Model -> Output = [traffic =large]

If this is the case, it is currently determining how to classify the

Input is called classification.

The output may be a scalar that is real world (output a few):

Input [temperature=20] -> Model -> Output = [traffic =300]

When this is true, it's referred to as regression.

## Classification

Classification can be used to group data points into segments. Machine Learning is utilized to discover the principles that describe how to separate data points.

But are the rules that were magically created? There are principles to be discovered by tactics. All of them focus on utilizing replies and data to discover principles that linearly data points.

Linear is a fundamental notion in machine learning. That separability means it is 'will'? So put classification approaches attempt to get the ideal method to divide data points.

The lines are called decision boundaries. It is called the chosen surface. The conclusion defines that when a data point falls inside its borders, it'll be assigned a particular course.

## Regression

Regression is another kind of learning. The difference between regression and classification is that regression sparks a number as opposed to a course. Regression is helpful when calling the fever for any day, number-based issues like stock exchange costs, or the likelihood of an event.

## Cases

Regression is used to find the routines in stocks to determining when to buy/sell and earn a profit, and other resources. For instance, if it is spam, it's currently being used to classify.

Both regression learning and of the classification techniques may be extended to tasks. By way of instance, tasks involving sound and language. Classification, object chatbots, and detection are a few examples.

A current example uses model supervised learning to virtually videos of people.

You may be wondering how this job can relate to regression or classification? It comes back to all in the world is clarified with numbers and mathematics. In this instance, there is a neural network still currently outputting numbers, such as in regression. But the amounts will be a mesh's numerical 3d values.

## Unsupervised Learning

In learning, enter information is provided in the examples. But it might be surprising to know it is possible to discover intricate and intriguing patterns hidden.

An example of learning in real life could be sorting color coins. Nobody taught you how you could separate them, but it is possible to see which color coins are related and cluster them by looking at their attributes like color.

An unsupervised learning algorithm (t-SNE) properly clusters handwritten digits to classes, based solely on their features,

This type of Learning may be supervised. Learning the elimination of oversight means that the issue is becoming less defined. The algorithm includes an idea of what patterns to search for.

Should you learned to perform with the by re-using the understanding of notes, rhythms, and chords, you would learn. But if you taught yourself, then you would find it much harder knowing where to begin.

By being unsupervised, you, at a fashion, begin from a clean slate with prejudice and could find a problem to be solved by a new approach. That is the reason why learning can be called knowledge discovery. When conducting data analysis, education is helpful.

We utilize to locate the structures in data density estimation. The most frequent type of that is clustering. There are latent factor models, reduction, and detection. Unsupervised techniques demand networks such as deep conditioning networks and auto-encoders, but we will not go to this launch site.

## Clustering

Learning is used for grouping. Clustering is the action of producing groups. Clustering attempts to come across subgroups. We're not limited to some set of tags as this can be unsupervised learning and therefore are free to choose the number of clusters to make. That is both a curse and a benefit. Selecting a version that has the right amount of groups (sophistication) needs to be run through an empirical design selection procedure

## Anomaly Detection

The identification of unusual or infrequent items that differ from the vast majority of information. For example, your lender will use this to discover fraudulent activity on your card. Your spending habits will collapse inside a reasonable range of values and behaviors. But to slip from you with your card that the action will differ from your typical pattern. Anomaly Detection uses unsupervised learning to discover and to separate these odd occurrences.

## Dimensionality Reduction

Reduction aims to find the most significant features to decrease the attribute put down into a much smaller group which encodes the data.

For example, in forecasting the amount of traffic every day of the week, month, and a variety of events scheduled for this day as inputs shown. However, the month may be for predicting the amount of traffic not crucial.

Machine learning cans confound Algorithms and also make them accurate and efficient. Just the most crucial attributes are used and identified by using reduction. Principal Component Analysis (PCA) is a widely used technique.

# Cases

In the actual world, clustering has been used to by exploring what subgroups of celebrity's form dependent on the qualities of the personality, Find a new kind of character. It is utilized into groups based on attributes and their behaviors.

Association learning is employe for discovering or advocating associated products. A frequent instance is market basket analysis. In market basket analysis, association rules can be found to forecast things. Amazon uses this. They urge items if you put a notebook on your basket.

Anomaly detection is ideal for situations like fraud Detection and malware detection.

## Semi-supervised learning

Learning is a mixture of unsupervised approaches. The learning procedure isn't closely supervised, such as outputs for each input signal, but we also do not allow the algorithm to do its thing and supply no kind of comments. Studying takes the road. It can combine a small amount of data. Using a considerable dataset, it decreases the load of getting labeled data. It opens up a lot of issues to be solved using machine learning.

## Generative Adversarial Networks

Generative Adversarial Networks (GANs) are a recent Breakthrough with results. GANs utilize a generator, two networks, and a discriminator. The generator also creates the discriminator and output critiques it. They become skilled by fighting against each other.

Using a system to create input and a different one to generate outputs, there isn't any requirement for us to present each time to labels, and thus, it could be hail.

## Cases

There is a perfect illustration in scans, for example, breast cancer scans. There is a trained specialist necessary to tag these that are costly and time-consuming. Instead, a specialist may label only a little pair of breastfeeding scans. Also, the semi-supervised algorithm would be able to leverage this small subset and use it to some more significant group of scans.

A neural network called a GAN (generative adversarial system) could be utilized to synthesize images, without using labeled training data.

## Reinforcement Learning

The kind of machine learning is my favorite. It is more complicated and familiar, but it generated incredible outcomes. It does not utilize tags as such and uses benefits to learn.

You'll have heard of if you are knowledgeable about the psychology of reinforcement learning. Otherwise, you understand the idea of how we know from life. Within this approach, negative and positive comments are utilized to reinforce behaviors. Consider it like training a puppy; the right actions are rewarded with a prize and eventually become more prevalent. Corrupt practices eventually become common and are penalized. This behavior is crucial in reinforcement learning.

This is similar to the way we as people learn. We learn from them and get negative and positive signs. The compounds in our minds are among several ways. When something great happens, the nerves in our brains offer a reach of favorable neurotransmitters like dopamine that makes us feel great, and we become prone to repeat that particular activity. We do not require constant supervision to understand, such as in learning. By merely giving the occasional reinforcement signs, we nevertheless learn quite effectively.

Among the elements of Reinforcement Learning is that it's a first step apart from coaching on stationary datasets, and rather than having the ability to work with lively, noisy data-rich surroundings. This brings Machine Learning nearer into a learning style. The world is our atmosphere that is complicated.

Games are well-identified in Reinforcement Learning research. They supply perfect environments that are data-rich. The scores in matches are classic reward signs to train behaviors. Time could haul up in-game surroundings that were simulated to decrease the training period.

A Reinforcement Learning algorithm aims to optimize it's by playing the game over and over again Rewards. If you're able to frame an issue with a regular 'score' as a reward, then it's very likely to be suited to Reinforcement Learning.

## Cases

Learning has not been utilized in the real because it is complicated and new to the world. However, a real-world illustration is using reinforcement learning how to reduce data center running costs by controlling the heating systems in a better manner. The algorithm finds an optimum coverage to find the energy expenses of how to behave.

In matches, it is utilized in research. Games of Ideal information (where you may observe the whole state of the surroundings) and incomplete data (where portions of this country are concealed, e.g., the actual world) have seen an unbelievable achievement that outperforms people.

# CHAPTER 2
# ADVANTAGES OF MACHINE LEARNING

## 10 WAYS IN WHICH MACHINE LEARNING CAN HELP YOUR BUSINESS

Machine learning (ML) extracts significant insights from raw information to solve complicated small business issues. ML algorithms let computers to come across unique kinds of insights that are concealed without being explicitly programmed to do so and learn in your information iteratively. ML is currently growing at a pace that is rapid and is being driven by new computing technology.

Machine Assists in improving business Scalability and Enhancing Business Operations:

ML calculations and artificial intelligence tools have gained popularity for this purpose.

Organizations can profit by understanding how machine learning can use by companies and execute that method.

## 10 Business Benefits of Machine Learning

ML helps in extracting data. If employed in the ideal fashion, ML can function as a remedy to many different company intricacies issues, and predict complex customer behaviors. We also have seen several significant technology giants, such as Google, Amazon, Microsoft, etc. coming up with their Cloud Machine Learning platforms.

A number of critical ways that ML can help your company records here:

## Customer Lifetime Value Prediction

Customer lifetime segmentation and value forecast are a few of the challenges faced by entrepreneurs. Firms have access to a large quantity of information, which can be used to derive small business insights that are significant. ML and data mining may help companies predict customer behaviors, buying patterns, and aid in delivering the very best possible offers to individual clients, according to their surfing and purchase histories.

## Predictive Maintenance

It is followed by manufacturing firms and maintenance practices that are inefficient and costly. However, businesses in this field can take advantage of ML to find patterns and insights. It assists in reducing the dangers related to sudden failures, and this is referred to as care and removes unnecessary expenditures. ML architecture could be constructed using workflow visualization programs, information, more analysis surroundings, as well as also the feedback loop.

## Eliminates Manual Data Entry

Incorrect and Copy data are a few of the most significant problems faced by companies. ML and modeling calculations can avoid any errors. ML apps make by employing the data that originate these procedures better. Hence, precisely the time can be utilized by the workers for executing jobs that add value.

## Discovering Spam

The machine in identifying spam, learning has been in use for quite some time. Email service providers made use of rule-based tactics to filter spam out. By using neural networks to detect malware and spam messages, spam blockers are generating guidelines.

## Product Recommendations

This can help in developing product-based learning and can improve recommendation systems. The majority of the sites nowadays are using a machine. Here, the ML algorithms utilize a client's purchase history and fit it to identify patterns and groups. These goods are suggested to clients inspiring product purchases.

## Fiscal Analysis

With historic and large quantities of quantitative information, ML can utilize it for the analysis. ML is used in the fund for loan underwriting trading, portfolio management, and fraud detection. Future applications of ML in finance may comprise conversational interfaces and Chatbots for opinion analysis, client support, and safety.

## Picture Thumbnails

This is known as computer vision recognition. It can create symbolic and numeric information from pictures and other data that is high-dimensional. It entails ML data mining, pattern recognition, and database knowledge discovery. ML in picture recognition is an important facet and can use by firms in various industries such as health care, cars, etc.

## Medical Diagnosis

Health care organizations have been helped by ML in diagnosis to enhance the individual's health and reduce health expenses, using superior instruments and treatment strategies. It predicts readmissions and is currently utilize to generate identification, urge medications, and identify high-risk sufferers. Advice and these predictions are drawn with data and records collections together with the symptoms.

## Enhancing Cyber Security

ML can utilize to increase an organization's safety. Cybersecurity is just one of the issues. Here, Ml lets new-generation suppliers construct technology, which efficiently and rapidly detects dangers.

## Growing Customer Satisfaction

ML guarantee and helps in enhancing customer loyalty client

experience. Employing the call records achieves this and, based on the customer requirement, will be assigned to an adequate customer support. This reduces the time spent on customer relationships and the price. Because of this, major organizations utilize calculations to supply hints to their clients.

# 6 Machine Learning Benefits That Are Making a Change for Firms

Machine Learning (ML) is a branch of Artificial Intelligence (AI) that's revolutionizing the office. It describes the practice of creating calculations that are self-learning utilizing data input signals. The objective of machine learning is to boost precision. It does so by maximizing the operation of a job from expertise obtained with conducting through datasets that are associated.

Any progress of a purpose to the accuracy provides a world of advantages -- notably concerning the business. What advantages are we referring to just? Keep Reading to learn:

## 1. Client Behavior Prediction

A more in-depth investigation of Consumer habits can provide invaluable insight into their patterns. Inferences precise as to a client opts for service, or a single product might produce. Machine learning highlights these findings at a quicker rate than investigation. Furthermore, this may also help the customer demand forecast further improves.

## 2. Menial's Conclusion Tasks

Data entry errors can prove to be costly mistakes. This price tag isn't confine to the direct cost of adjusting them. It may damage the client's business and retention authenticity, to not mention any loss of earnings or reimbursement expenses. Its precision saves money and time, in employing ML to data entry jobs.

Furthermore, worker job to improve by lightening the load of work assignments offering stimulation that is little-to-no Satisfaction is. Data entry is one of the responsibilities that everyone will be delighted to see removed in their lists. Subsequently, businesses can love improvements in staff productivity while having the ability to channel more resources and time to other, more lucrative pursuits.

## 3. Increased Sales Opportunities

It is essential to check into any to identify sales prospects' marketing problems and refine your consumer profiles to address your business' target market. This entails digging into the user journeys of new, existing, or returning clients. Companies acquire insight they can advocate, in assessing this part of the expertise.

A recent poll found that over 75 percent of businesses generating over half a million dollars in earnings say they experienced a more significant increase. AI applications optimize recommendations and base their learnings on the data offered. These may be easily integrated as up-sale or cross-sale chances.

## 4. Insightful Business Intelligence

Among the keys to success in business will be currently identifying the selling factors and their advantages as compared with the contest. This clear-sightedness is the thing that helps convey a business' value proposition. Hypotheses analyzed utilizing data to offer recommendations for business choices, and it can use to create them.

## 5. Improved Customer Satisfaction

Machine learning algorithms can collate the Information, examine it, and linked using a service or product. It may program to the departments to client questions. This automation supplies solution that is quicker and reduces client wait times that are a difficulty. Both these aspects lead to customer satisfaction, which can help strengthen referrals in addition to build a loyal customer base.

## 6. Smarter Workplaces

Assistants, such as EVA by Voice, are currently creating waves at the office -- and rightly so! They enhance efficacy for office jobs like scheduling meetings and transcribing meeting minutes. Their capacity is characteristic.

The use of machine learning to Automatic Speech recognition (ASR) instruction is paramount for improving precision. With increased accuracy in their functionality, the workflow is much more compact, and companies can function with greater efficiency in addition to a stronger adherence to stricter privacy regulations.

## Putting Speech Data to Work

In supplying transcription solutions, create many top-quality speech information. Through system learning, we can continually enhance the precision with. Besides, we provide the maximum quality confirmed and human-annotated training places for speech recognition training and machine learning. These capacities can implement through languages, accents, and some other information points your company might need.

# 8 Ways Businesses Can Benefit from Machine Learning

With the buzz around data that is large, artificial Intelligence, and machine learning (ML), businesses are currently becoming curious about the applications and advantages of system learning in a company. A good deal of folks have heard of ML, but do not understand the value it could add to your own company, or just what it is, what problems it could solve. ML is a data evaluation procedure that leverages ML algorithms help with no programmed computers locate insights and to learn from the information.

With Google, Amazon, and Microsoft Azure, we have observed ML and intelligence gaining prominence. Without being aware of it, we have all seen ML. A number of the most frequent cases are 'Spam' detection by your provider, also 'Picture' or 'Face' tagging performed by Facebook. While Gmail admits the chosen words or the routine to filter out junk, Facebook mechanically tags uploaded pictures using the picture (face) recognition procedure. The company's advantages of ML and AI are numerous.

## Best 8 Business Advantages of Machine Learning

Let us examine a few of the ML and business benefits, beginning with all the sales and advertising industry.

## Simplifies Product Marketing and Assists in Accurate Sales Forecasts

ML assists businesses in ways to market their products, create sales, and better calculations. ML offers enormous benefits to the sales and advertising industry.

## Enormous Data Presence from Unlimited Resources

ML consumes several comprehensive data. The data can be used to alter and examine your sales and promotion strategies based on client patterns. Once you trained your model, then it is going to have the ability to identify exceptionally relevant factors. You will have the ability to receive targeted by preceding complex, and lengthy integrations data feeds.

## Quick Analysis Prediction and Performance

The rate at that ML defines relevant and consumes information makes it possible that you take action. For example, ML will maximize the most effective offer for your clients. As a result, the client will have the ability to observe the ideal deal at a specified time, without you investing time to program and make the perfect ad observable for your clients.

## Interpret Past Client Behaviors

ML will allow you to examine the information related to behaviors that are previous or results. Depending on the distinct and new data, you'll have the ability to earn predictions of client behaviors.

## Facilitates Accurate Medical Predictions and Diagnoses

In the healthcare sector, ML helps, in identification that is easy for wounded, makes diagnoses, recommends the most excellent medications, and forecasts readmissions. These are dependent on the symptoms in addition to the datasets of individual documents. Diagnoses and medication recommendations will facilitate patient recovery with no need for drugs. This manner, ML makes it feasible to increase health at prices in the sector.

## Simplifies Time-Intensive Documentation in Data Entry

Inaccuracy and data duplication would be the significant problems. Well, this scenario can enhance by machine learning algorithms and modeling. For this, machines may execute data entry jobs that are time-intensive, leaving your resources that are proficient free to concentrate on additional duties that are value-adding.

26

## Improves Truth of Financial Rules and Designs

ML has a substantial effect on the finance industry. Some of the machine learning advantages include above all trading, loan underwriting, and portfolio management fraud detection. According to a report, 'The Future of Underwriting' ML facilitates data evaluations for assessing and discovering nuances and anomalies. This assists in improving the accuracy of principles and units.

## Easy Spam Detection

Spam detection was among the earliest issues ML. A couple of years back, suppliers utilize rule-based tactics to filter spam out. But spam blockers are currently creating rules employing networks to remove spam emails. The systems comprehend by assessing the principles across a network of 19, phishing messages, and spam email.

## Increases the Performance of Predictive Care in the Manufacturing Industry

Manufacturing companies have preventative in addition to correct maintenance practices. These are inefficient and costly, and at this point, ML comes with assistance. ML will help in the development of effective maintenance programs that are predictive. Following predictive care programs will minimize the odds of failures reducing maintenance actions.

## Better Client Segmentation and Accurate Lifetime Value Prediction

Life value forecast and client segmentation will be some of the latest challenges faced by entrepreneurs. Advertising units and sales may have enormous quantities of data, such as email campaigns, site traffic, and data. Right predictions for advertising offer that was individual and incentives can attain with ML. Savvy marketers use ML to eliminate guesswork related to online affiliate advertising. As an example, by using the data representing the pattern of a group of users throughout a trial 20, companies will be helped in forecasting the likelihood of conversion into a version. A version causes customer interventions to persuade customers to convert and to engage the consumers from the trial.

## Recommending the Ideal Product

Item recommendation is also an essential aspect of any revenue and marketing plan, such as cross-selling and upselling. ML versions based on which they identify these products from the merchandise stock and will examine the purchase history of a client. The algorithm will set goods and will identify patterns. This practice is referred to like learning, and it can be a kind of ML algorithm. This kind of model will make it possible for companies to create product recommendations that are better for their client's inspiring product purchases. This manner, learning assists in making a superior recommendation strategy.

The machine is made by these programs invention fad. ML enables companies to seamlessly discover patterns and trends from data sets that are varied and large. Firms are now able to automate research to translate human company interactions, which have been performed by people, to carry actions; this enables enterprises to provide personalized, fresh, or differentiated products and solutions. Contemplating ML as a tactical initiative may be a choice. But business risks might be carried by the installation. It is far better to approach investment choices.

## What Are the Advantages and Disadvantages of Machine Learning?

Machine learning abilities are the most innovative technology by the analytics engines. It produces buying recommendations on Amazon, employed in antivirus and security applications. Just like any type of technology, it is not perfect, although there are several advantages of machine learning. Let's examine the advantages and disadvantages of machine learning and how they can impact the goals of your company and you.

Pro: Trends and Patterns Are Identify with Sudden

A machine learning advantage concerns this tech's Capability to examine large volumes of information and identify trends and patterns which may not be evident to a person. As an example, a machine learning application can pinpoint a causal connection between two events: this creates the technology effective at data mining, especially. The ability to correctly and rapidly identify patterns or trends is just one of the benefits of machine learning.

Con: There is a High Degree of Error Susceptibility

A mistake can lead to havoc as most of the occasions following the error could be skewed, faulty, or just undesirable. Errors do happen, and it is a susceptibility that programmers have been not able to premeditate and negate. These errors may take several forms, which change based on the manner in. As an example, you may have a detector that creates a faulty data collection. The data could feed the machine learning application which uses it and could lead to results in the output of the algorithm. The outcome might be a circumstance where merchandise recommendations that are related aren't comparable or related. Thus, you may have pet bowls, beach towels, and apparel contained in the same batch of "associated" product recommendations. A computer gets the capability to realize that these items aren't in any manner where intellect is necessary; this is.

Errors are debatable with the independent machine character of the autonomous technology. You conduct a machine since you don't need a human learning application: this usually means an error might not discover. Once the issue is recognized, it may have a decent amount of attempt and time to root out the origin of the situation. And you have to implement measures cure and to fix the mistake.

Machine learning proponents assert the Diagnosis and correction procedure is much superior to the choices in regards to efficiency and productivity. Simply by reviewing data, this position can be shown in several situations.

On a related note, machine truths, which may differ from literal truths. It's essential when utilizing machine learning that your account for that fact.

Pros: Machine Learning Enhances Over Time

Among the benefits of machine learning algorithms Is their capacity. Precision and efficiency thanks typically improve to its ever-increasing amounts: this provides the program or algorithm more "encounter," which may, in turn, use to make improved predictions or decisions.

A fantastic example of this advancement over time entails weather forecast models. Studying events and weather patterns makes predictions. The more info you have a collection, the larger the precision of a prediction that is certain. This is also true for calculations used to make recommendations or conclusions.

Con: It could take time (and Resources) for machine learning how to bring results

Since machine learning happens as a result of, over the years, exposure to enormous data collections, there might be a time once interface or the algorithm isn't developed sufficiently for your requirements.

To put it differently, machine learning requires time you've limited computing power. Running computer models and managing volumes of information stinks up lots of computing power, which may be expensive. Before turning into machine learning, it is essential to think about if you may spend the amount of time or cash necessary to develop the technologies where it's going to be helpful. The quantity of time required will vary based on the information source, the data's essence and their use. It's sensible to get help from an expert in data mining and machine.

You should consider if you will need to await new Information to produce. As an example, you may have the power on Earth where power will do nothing to accelerate the evolution of a weather forecast algorithm since there's simply so much data, and you'll finally reach a stage. As information is create -- something which may take days, weeks, months, or years, you will simply wait.

In a sense, this Procedure is like the training interval required to get a new worker. Though, a machine learning engine place in its notice and cannot walk in your office.

Pros: Machine Learning Lets You Adapt Without Individual Intervention

This technology allows for adaptation that is prompt, without the requirement for intervention: this is only one of the advantages of the machine.

A superb example of this can originate in safety and anti-virus software applications, which AI technologies and leverage machine learning to execute filters and defenses to dangers.

These programs use machine learning on how to identify dangers and tendencies. AI technologies execute the steps that were right for shielding or neutralizing against this threat. Machine learning has removed the difference between the times when a hazard is detected. When a reply is issued time, this answer is essential in a market where hackers, viruses, worms, spiders can affect thousands or perhaps millions of individuals in minutes.

Pros and Con: Automation

Machine learning is an integral element in technology, such as analytics and intelligence. Machine learning's nature implies as analysts and programmers have been freed up to carry out jobs a computer can't manage; it could save you money and time.

On the flip side, you have a computer that is sure to create any developer squirm. For the time being, technology is imperfect. There are workarounds. As an example, if you are employing machine learning technologies to be able to come up with an algorithm, then you may plan the machine learning port, so it indicates changes or improvements that have to be implemented by an individual.

This workaround adds the equation and a gatekeeper when a computer is responsible for eliminating the possibility of issues that could arise. When it is put to practice after all might not operate. If your machine is configured to automatically execute improvements that are suggested from the machine learning port, surgeries can run off the rails until a person intervenes, describes the issue, and requires corrective steps.

Like most technology, machine learning is not appropriate for each business or every program. The advantages and disadvantages of technology will be different from your objectives. But there are lots of companies that would like a benefit from machine learning and associated technologies like analytics and AI. Seven Tablets will help should you fall into the latter category. Our world-class group of programmers specializes in lots of the most recent technology, such as machine learning, blockchain, predictive analytics, augmented reality, virtual reality, artificial intelligence, and natural language processing.

# CHAPTER 3

# MACHINE LEARNING CATEGORIES

Researchers began out with explaining Supervised Learning: this is the event of the home cost prediction mentioned in the paper above.

Scientists found that it does the task; they concluded reinforcement learning, and that the way, the machine was rewarded.

Quite soon is now huge that the methods developed so far neglected supply us the forecasts and to examine the huge data.

From the Artificial Neural Networks (ANN) generated within our binary computers, we came to learn about simulation.

The machine learns with the computing electricity and memory tools which are available now.

It is proved that deep learning has solved a lot of unsolvable issues.

The technique is by providing incentives with advanced into deep learning networks, and there comes deep reinforcement learning.

Let's now study all one of those categories in detail.

## Supervised Learning

Learning is comparable to training a kid to walk. You may hold the child's hand, show him how to shoot his foot forwards, walk to get a demonstration, and so forth till the child learns to walk by himself.

## Regression

In the case of learning, you give illustrations that were known by definite. You state that for given characteristic worth x1, the output signal is y1, for x2 is y2, etc. According to this information, you allow the computer to determine an empirical connection between x and y.

When the system is trained in this manner with a sufficient amount of data points, you would ask the device to predict Y for a given X. Assuming you know the actual value of Y with this X, you'll have the ability to deduce if the machine's forecast is accurate.

You will test if the machine has discovered by utilizing the test information. When you're satisfied that the system can perform the predictions using a desirable level of precision (say 80 to 90 percent), you can stop additional coaching the machine.

You can use the system to perform on the predictions data request the machine to predict Y for a given X for which you don't know the worth of Y or points. This practice comes, we spoke.

# Classification

You may utilize machine learning methods for classification issues. To one group, you categorize objects of character in classification problems. As an instance, in some 100 student's states, you might like to set them into three classes according to their peaks - short, medium, and extended-term. Assessing every student's height, you may place them at a group.

When a student comes in, you may put him within aby measuring his height set. You'll train the system by following the principles from regression instruction. After the machine accomplishes forming the band, it is going to have the ability to classify any unknown new pupil correctly. You would use the evaluation data to confirm that the device has discovered your method of classification before placing the version that is developed in creation.

Where the AI started its supervised learning is a journey. This technique was implemented in many scenarios. You've used this version while doing precisely the hand-written recognition in your machine. Several algorithms are developed for learning that you are going to learn about them.

## Unsupervised Learning

In learning, we do not define a goal Factor into the machine. Instead, we ask the device, "What do you tell me?". More importantly, we might ask questions like, given a massive data collection X, "Which are the five greatest classes we could use X?"

Or "What attributes occur together most often in X?". To arrive at the answers to these queries, you can realize that the number of data points which the machine will need to deduce a plan would be quite large. With about a few tens of thousands of data points, the system may be trained in the case of learning.

Nonetheless, in the case of unsupervised learning, the amount of data points that are reasonably suitable for learning begins at a couple million. Nowadays, information is usually abundantly offered. The information requires curating. The number of information that's continuously flowing into an information curation is a hopeless undertaking.

The next figure shows the border between the yellow and dots determined by machine learning. You may view it as the machine would have the ability to ascertain the course of all those dots that are black.

## Reinforcement Learning

Think about training an; we instruct our furry friend Chunk to us. We ask your dog to bring it back and toss the ball. Each time the puppy does this correctly, we reward the dog. The puppy learns that he is given a benefit by doing the work, and the puppy begins doing the job each time. Correctly, this idea is put from the "Reinforcement" form of learning. The method was designed to play with matches. The machine is provided with an algorithm to test all probable moves. The computer may choose among those motions. The device is rewarded differently if the transfer is correct or it might be penalized. The system will begin following several iterations will learn how to address the match puzzle with a precision that is greater and differentiating between moves. The truth of winning the match will improve since the machine performs more and more games.

## Sport Puzzle

This method of machine learning and the difference in Assessing learning that you don't need to provide the input/output pairs that were tagged. The focus is about finding the balance between researching versus harnessing the learning alternatives, the alternatives.

## Deep Learning

Learning is a version based on Artificial Neural Networks (ANN), more especially Convolutional Neural Networks (CNN)s. There are lots of architectures utilized in learning, such as belief networks that are profound, neural networks, recurrent networks, and neural networks.

These networks are successfully employed in solving issues of medical image analysis, speech recognition, natural language processing, bioinformatics, drug design, computer vision, and matches. There are numerous areas in. Learning demands humongous information and processing capacity, which is easily available nowadays.

## Deep Reinforcement Learning

Deep Reinforcement Learning (DRL) joins the techniques of Profound and reinforcement learning. With learning to make a DRL model, the reinforcement learning algorithms are united. The method was in the fields of robotics, video games, finance, and health with fantastic achievements. Producing DRL versions now solves many problems. There's a lot of research, and the businesses can actively pursue this.

You have got a brief introduction; let us explore deeper.

# Kinds of Machine Learning Algorithms You Have to Know

## Types of machine learning Algorithms

There several variations of the way to specify the types of machine learning algorithms, but generally they can be divided into classes according to their purpose that are the following:

- Supervised learning

- Unsupervised Learning

- Semi-supervised Learning

- Reinforcement Learning

## Supervised Learning

I love to consider learning that is supervised together with the idea of function approximation: mainly, we train an algorithm and to select the function which best describes the input information, the one which for a specified X gets the ideal estimation of y (X -> y). The majority of the time, people are unable to work out the original purpose that makes the correct predictions and yet another reason is that the algorithm depends upon an assumption made by people about the way the computer must learn. Those assumptions introduce a prejudice; bias is the subject I will explain in another article.

Here the pros act as the instructor Computer with training information comprising the input/predictors, and we reveal it that the appropriate replies (output) and by the data, the computer ought to have the ability to learn the routines.

Learning algorithms attempt to simulate relationships and dependencies between the input and the goal prediction output attributes such that we can forecast the output signal values for information based on those customs that it learned in the data collections.

Publish

Predictive Model

We've labeled data

The Kinds of supervised learning issues include regression and classification issues

List of Algorithms

Nearest Neighbor

Naive Bayes

Decision Trees

Linear Regression

Support Vector Machines (SVM)

Neural Networks

Unsupervised Learning

Data train the computer.

Here there is no teacher at all the computer may. After it learns patterns in data, 15, Can teach you items Algorithms a helpful in scenarios what to search for in the information.

## Descriptive Model

The Kinds of learning algorithms comprise Association and algorithms rule learning algorithms.

## List of Algorithms
## Semi-supervised Learning

Either no label for the dataset observations is found, or tags for all of the observations are found. Learning falls in between two cases and needs skilled experts to do that, in most scenarios, with a high-cost tagging; therefore, although in the lack of labels in nearly all the observations, algorithms are the top candidates to the model construction. These methods exploit the concept that although the team members of the unlabeled data are unknown, this information carries important information regarding the group parameters.

## Reinforcement Learning

The System targets utilizing observations Interaction with the surroundings to take or decrease the threat. The reinforcement learning algorithm (known as the representative) continuously learns in the surroundings iteratively. Until it explores the assortment of states that are feasible in the procedure, the agent learns from its own experiences of the surroundings.

Reinforcement Learning Is a kind and, of machine learning; thus, a branch of artificial intelligence. It helps software agents and machines to ascertain the behavior to be able to maximize its functionality. Straightforward reward feedback is needed to understand its behavior.

There are a specific sort of difficulty defines Reinforcement Learning, and of its alternatives are called Reinforcement Learning algorithms. In the issue, a broker is supposed to determine the actions to pick according to his condition. The point is referred to as a Markov Decision Process if this measure is repeated.

To be able to produce smart programs (also known as Brokers), reinforcement learning goes through these measures:

The broker observes the input condition.

The purpose is used to make the broker act.

The broker receives a reward Following the action is done or reinforcement from the environment.

Information Regarding the reward's set is stored.

List of Algorithms

Q-Learning

Temporal Difference (TD)

Deep Adversarial Networks

## Use cases

Some programs of this reinforcement Are computer played games (Chess, Move), robotic hands, and self-driving automobiles)

There's likely to use unique criteria to classify Kinds of machine learning algorithms. However, I believe using the learning endeavor is excellent to visualize the large picture of ML and that I think under your issue and the information you need in hand, it is simple to determine if you'll utilize Supervised, unsupervised, or reinforcement learning. In the articles, I will provide examples of every kind of machine learning algorithm.

## Different Kinds of Learning in Machine Learning

Machine learning is Inherits ideas from related disciplines like artificial intelligence.

This field's focus is studying, that is, getting skills or knowledge inexperience; this implies synthesizing theories.

There are lots of distinct kinds of learning which you may

experience as a professional in the area of machine learning to practices out of fields of research.

## Kinds of Learning

Given the focus on the field of machine learning is "learning," that there are lots of types that you might encounter as a professional.

Some kinds of learning explain subfields of this analysis comprised of several distinct sorts of algorithms, such as "learning" Other people explain powerful techniques that you could use in your projects, for example, "transfer learning."

There are of learning which you have to be 14 Kinds Familiar with as a system learning pro; they're:

Learning Issues

· Supervised Learning

· Unsupervised Learning

· Reinforcement Learning

· Hybrid Learning Issues

· Semi-Supervised Learning

· Self-Supervised Learning

· Multi-Instance Learning

· Statistical Inference

- Inductive Learning

- Deductive Inference

- Transudative Learning

- Learning Techniques

- Multi-Task Learning

- Active Learning

- Online Learning

- Transfer Learning

- Ensemble Learning

In the next sections, we'll have a look at each in turn.

Did I overlook an important kind of learning?

Allow me to know in the comments below.

## Learning Issues

We will have a look learning issue in machine learning.

## 1. Supervised Learning

Supervised learning refers to a class of problems that Involves using a version to find out the mapping between the goal variable and input cases.

Models are inserted on training information outputs and used to make predictions on test places where the inputs are supplied. The outputs in the model are to withheld target factors and utilized to gauge the ability of this model.

There are two kinds of learning issues that are supervised: they are classification that entails predicting regression and a class tag that entails calling a value.

An example of a classification problem is the MNIST Handwritten digits dataset in which the inputs are images of handwritten digits (pixel information), and the output signal is a class label for that which digit the picture represents (figures 0 to 9).

An example of a regression problem is the Boston home Costs dataset in which the inputs are factors that describe the output, and a locality signal is a home cost.

Some machine is described as "supervised" machine learning algorithms since they are created for supervised machine learning issues. Popular examples include support vector machines, decision trees, and more.

Algorithms are known as "supervised" since they Learn by creating predictions given cases of input information, and the versions are supervised and adjusted via an algorithm to better forecast the anticipated goal outputs in the training dataset.

Some calculations may be designed for classification (for example, logistic regression) or regression (like linear regression), and some might be used for both kinds of issues with slight alterations (like artificial neural networks).

# 2. Unsupervised Learning

Unsupervised learning refers to a class of problems that Involves using a version extract or describing relationships in data.

Compared to learning, unsupervised learning Works without outputs or goal factors upon the input. As such, learning doesn't have a teacher adjusting the design, as in the case of learning.

There are various kinds of learning that is, though there are they're clustering that entails discovering groups in density estimation and the information which involves outlining data's supply.

Density Estimation: Unsupervised learning difficulty, which Involves summarizing data's supply.

Where Delta an example of a clustering algorithm is k-Means refers to find from the information. A good illustration of a density estimation algorithm is Kernel Density Estimation, which entails using small groups of information samples that are related to estimating the supply for points.

Density and clustering estimation could be performed to find out about the patterns from the information.

Additional methods may be used, for example, a visualization that entails plotting or graphing data in projection techniques and various ways that involve reducing the dimensionality of this information.

An example of a visualization method could be a scatter plot. A good illustration of a projection system would be Primary Component Analysis that entails summarizing a dataset together with dependencies concerning eigenvalues and eigenvectors.

## 3. Reinforcement Learning

Learning refers to a class of problems where an agent learns to work with opinions and to operate within an environment.

Using an environment means that there's no stationary training dataset, opinions about performance toward the objective, and instead of a goal or set of goals that an agent must achieve, activities they could perform.

It's similar to learning, even though the feedback might be postponed and noisy, which makes it hard for a model or the broker to link cause and effect.

An example of a psychologist's difficulty is currently playing with a match where the broker has the objective of obtaining a score that is top and will make movements in the match and received opinions concerning rewards or punishments.

Impressive outcomes include using reinforcement at Google's at out-performing, the planet's top move participant AlphaGo.

Some examples of reinforcement learning algorithms comprise Q-learning learning and profound reinforcement learning.

Hybrid Learning Issues

The lines between supervised and unsupervised learning are

Blurry, and there are.

We will have a look common hybrid area of research: self-supervised semi-supervised and learning.

## 4. Semi-Supervised Learning

Learning is supervised in which the learning training information also contains a high number of examples and very few examples.

A learning model's objective would be to create utilization of each available data branded data such as in learning.

Making use of data might necessitate the use of Inspiration or of from techniques like density and clustering estimation. Supervised ideas or methods from learning could be utilized to label the examples or use labels to representations employed for prediction once patterns or groups are found.

It's typical for many learning that is real-world for tagging examples, Issues to be cases of learning issues given the computational or cost price. By way of instance, classifying photos needs a dataset of photos that have been tagged by operators.

Many issues from the fields of computer vision (picture info), natural language processing (text information), and automated speech recognition (sound information) fall into this class. They cannot be readily addressed with conventional supervised learning procedures.

# 5. Self-Supervised Learning

Learning identifies an unsupervised learning problem that's styled to apply supervised learning algorithms to resolve it.

Learning algorithms are used to resolve an alternative or pretext task; the result of that is a representation or model which may be utilized at the solution of the first (real) modeling issue.

A frequent example of learning Vision in which a corpus of unlabeled graphics is accessible and may be employed to train a design version, like making pictures grayscale and using a version forecast a color representation (colorization) or eliminating blocks of this picture and also have a version forecast the missing components (inpainting).

These are compressed or compact representations of the input. They reach this via a version that has a decoder component separated by a bottleneck, which reflects the inner representation of this input and an encoder.

Providing the input trains with these autoencoder versions requiring that the input reproduces encoding it to a representation trapping it back. The decoder is lost once trained, and the encoder can be used as required to make representations of the input.

Even though autoencoders are trained with a supervised learning process, an unsupervised learning difficulty is solved by them; they are a sort of projection way of reducing the dimensionality of input information.

Another case of learning is generative Adversarial GANs or networks. These models are frequently used for producing photographs using an assortment of examples name.

GAN versions are trained via another discriminator version that classifies illustrations of photographs from the domain name as real or imitation (created). The result can be fed back to upgrade the GAN version and invite it to create more realistic photographs on another iteration.

## 6. Multi-Instance Learning

Another issue that needs supervise is about groups or bags of samples that have been tagged, where individual cases are unlabeled.

Modeling involves utilizing the knowledge that some or one of the cases in a bag are correlated with a goal tag and also to forecast the tag for new totes in the future, given their makeup of numerous unlabeled examples.

Simple Procedures, like assigning class labels Utilizing and Cases learning algorithms that are regular work as a first step.

## Statistical Inference

Inference describes attaining at a conclusion or a result.

In machine fitting, a model learning and creating a forecast are both kinds of inference.

There are paradigms used as a frame for understanding some

learning issues that might be approached, or a few machine learning algorithms operate.

Some examples of methods for understanding are inductive, Deductive, and transitive inference and learning.

## 7. Inductive Learning

Learning entails using evidence to ascertain that the outcome.

Reasoning describes utilizing instances that are specific to determine general results, e.g., particular to the general.

Machine learning versions learn using a kind of inductive inference or inductive logic where overall principles (the version) are learned from particular historical examples (the information).

Adding a machine is a process of induction. The design is a generalization of the examples from the training dataset.

Theory or a model is made about the issue of training information: when this version is utilized, it's thought to hold over data.

## 8. Deductive Inference

Deductive or deduction inference describes utilizing overall Outcomes to be determined by Principles.

By comparing it with induction can be better understood by our deduction.

The deduction is the opposite of induction. If induction is moving to the overall from the particular, deduction is currently moving from the general to particular.

The deduction is All assumptions to be fulfilled before specifying the decision, whereas induction is a sort of reasoning which utilizes data that is available as proof for a result.

From the context of machine match, a model, the version may be used to produce predictions. This model's usage is a sort of deductive or deduction inference.

## 9. Transudative Learning

Transudative or transduction learning is used in the Area Illustrations were given by of learning theory to reference forecasting examples name.

It's different general principles from specific cases, e.g., special to particular.

Unlike induction, no generalization is demanded. Examples are utilized. This can be a problem than just induction.

An example of an algorithm would be that the neighbor's algorithm that doesn't mimic the training data but uses it each time.

For much more about the topic of transduction, visit the tutorial:

- Gentle Intro in Machine Learning to Transduction

- Contrasting Deduction, Induction, and Transduction:

We can contrast these three Kinds of inference context of machine learning.

## Learning Techniques

There is learning.

We will have a look at more procedures that are common:

these include active move and ensemble learning.

## 10. Multi-Task Learning

Learning Is a sort of supervised Involves a model that is matching on a single dataset that addresses relevant issues.

It entails devising Jobs in this manner that training improves the model's functioning around the tasks compared to being educated on any specific undertaking.

Learning can be a useful strategy for a single job, which may be shared with a different task with information that was tagged for by difficulty whenever there's a plethora of input information.

For instance, it's typical for a learning Issue that is multi-task to involve exactly the input patterns which supervised learning issues or could be used for distinct outputs. Within this installation, another area of the model may predict each output, letting the heart of the model to generalize every activity for the input signal.

A favorite example of really where the same multi-task learning is word embedding can be used to find out a representation of phrases from the text that's subsequently shared across all-natural language processing.

# 11. Active Learning

Learning is a method to resolve ambiguity through the learning 18, question a user operator throughout the learning process.

Learning seeks and is a sort of learning that is supervised to attain the same or better functionality of so-called "passive" supervised learning, though by becoming more efficient regarding what information is collected or utilized with this model.

It's not unreasonable to see active learning a method of solving an alternate paradigm for the kinds of issues, or learning issues.

Learning is a helpful approach when there isn't much Info available, and information is a costly tag or to collect. The learning procedure allows the sampling of the domain names to be led in a manner that optimizes the efficacy of the model and reduces the number of samples.

# 12. Online Learning

Learning entails using the information, and upgrading the version following the observation was created or before a prediction is a requirement.

Learning is suitable for all those issues where observations are in which the likelihood of distribution of observations is predicted to change over time and provided over time. The version is anticipated to change as often exploit and to catch those changes. Algorithms use this approach. More observations could fit into memory.

Normally, online learning attempts to minimize "regret," that is, the model performed in comparison to it may have done if the available information was accessible as a batch. One example of learning would be that the stochastic or gradient descent.

## 13. Transfer Learning

Transfer learning Is a sort of learning through which there is a version trained on a single job. Then all the version or a few is utilized as the beginning point for an endeavor that was related.

It's a useful method to issues. Related to the endeavor of also the task and interest has a lot of information.

Because the actions are, it's different from learning, whereas learning attempts performance, learned in motion learning considered tasks in precisely the same time in parallel by a version.

An illustration is an image in which a predictive classification Model, like an artificial neural network, may be trained onto a corpus of graphics. Also, the weights of this model may be utilized as a starting point when coaching to a dataset that was particular, like cats and dogs. The attributes discovered by design on the task, like pulling patterns and lines, will be useful on the brand-new undertaking that is related. Move learning is useful with as mentioned a present model, and versions that are trained may be used as a starting point, such as learning profound programs.

# 14. Ensemble Learning

Learning is an approach match on the forecasts from each version, and the data are combined. Ensemble learning aims to attain the performance of models compared to any version: this entails both determining the way to combine the forecasts and to make models. Learning is a helpful approach for enhancing the ability to decrease the variance of stochastic and also a problem domain learning algorithm, such as neural networks.

# CHAPTER 4-
# BIG DATA ANALYSIS TOOLS

## 11 Greatest Big Data Analytics Tools in 2020

Big Data Analytics applications utilize in supplying a meaningful evaluation of information. This program assists in discovering other info, customer preferences market trends.

Here are the 11 Top Big Data Analytics Tools with essential Attribute

## 1. Xplenty

Xplenty is an ETL solution data pipelines for data flows across a vast selection of destinations and resources. The robust transformation tools of plenty permit information normalize to wash and change while adhering to practices.

## Characteristics

Code-free, compelling data conversion offering

Rush API jack - pull information from any source which includes a hurry API

Destination flexibility - ship information to databases warehouses, and salesforce

Security - data masking and encryption to fulfill compliance requirements

Rush API - attain whatever possible on the Xplenty UI through the Xplenty API

A customer-centric firm that contributes to support

# 2. IDEA

Data Analysis Software is a comprehensive and easy-to-use data evaluation tool that assesses 100 percent of your information hastens doing data analytics to enable more successful and quicker audits and ensures data integrity. Since it's flexible, secure, enlightening, and repeatable Regular, over 500,000 professionals rely on IDEA ® Data Evaluation Software.

## Characteristics

Import data

Origin information integrity protected by accessibility

Use 100 audit works

Pinpoint outliers, styles, and designs

A clear audit trail allows for analysis that is repeatable.

## 3. Microsoft HDInsight

Azure HD Insight is a Hadoop and sparks support from the cloud. It supplies information cloud offerings in just two classes, standard, and premium. It provides an audience for the company to conduct its enormous information workloads.

## Characteristics

Reputable analytics

It provides monitoring and security.

Expand safety and protect data resources and governance controls into the cloud

A platform for scientists and programmers

Integration with productivity software

Deploy Hadoop from the cloud without buying hardware or paying additional up-front prices

## 4. Skytree

Skytree is a model that is accurate to be built by scientists. It gives precise system learning.

## Characteristics

Highly Scalable Algorithms

Artificial Intelligence for Data Researchers

It allows information scientists to comprehend and to visualize the logic behind ML conclusions.

Skytree through the GUI that is easy-to-adopt or even programmatically in Java

Model Interpretability

It designs to solve predictive difficulties preparation capabilities.

Programmatic and GUI Access

## 5. Talend

Talend is an excellent data tool that simplifies and automates Big Data integration. Its wizard generates code. Additionally, it allows data integration that is big, master data management, and assesses data quality.

## Characteristics

Accelerate time to value to large data jobs

Simplify ETL & ELT for data that is large

Information quality with natural and machine learning language processing

Data jobs that is large to accelerate

Streamline of the DevOps procedures

## 6. Splice Machine

Splice Machine is a vast data tool. Their structure is mobile across clouds like AWS, Azure, and Google.

## Characteristics

It may scale to tens of thousands of nodes from a few to enable applications at each scale

The Machine optimizer automatically questions into the

dispersedHBaseareas.

Reduce direction, deploy and reduce the danger

Consume deploy, test and develop machine learning models

## 7. Spark

Apache Spark is an open-source data that is a massive analytics tool. It provides more than 80 high-level operators, which makes it straightforward to construct parallel programs. It uses to process large datasets.

## Characteristics.

It helps to run a program in Hadoop cluster up to 100 Times quicker in memory and ten times quicker on disc

It provides lighting Quick Processing.

Support for Analytics

Ability to contain Hadoop and Present Hadoop Data

It offers APIs in Java, Scala, or even Python.

## 8. Plotly

Plotly is an application that lets users produce charts and dashboards.

## Characteristics

Turn any info into informative and eye-catching Images

It offers details to industries that audited information provenance.

Offers public Community strategy

## 9. Apache SAMOA

Apache SAMOA is a data analytics instrument that is huge. It empowers the growth of ML algorithms. It gives a selection of algorithms for machine learning jobs and data mining.

## 10. Lumify

It is an information fusion, visualization, and analysis platform. It assists users in research relationships in their information utilizing a suite of choices and to detect connections.

## Characteristics

It supplies 2D and 3D chart visualizations using a variety of automatic designs

It offers an assortment of options for assessing the links between things on the chart.

It Includes interface and specific processing components for textual content, pictures, and videos.

Its spaces feature permits you to arrange work jobs or workspaces.

It builds on proven data technologies.

## 11. Elasticsearch

Elasticsearch is an analytics and a data search engine. It's an analytics engine and a RESTful hunt for solving quantities of use cases. It gives maximum reliability scalability and management that is effortless.

## Characteristics

It lets combine various types of searches like structured, unstructured, geo, metric, etc

Intuitive APIs for direction and tracking give visibility and control.

It utilizes JSON and RESTful APIs. Additionally, it assembles and maintains customers in several languages, such as Java, Python, NET, and Groovy.

Elasticsearch-Hadoop Analytics and Search feature to manage huge data.

It provides experience with safety reporting and machine learning attributes.

## 12. R-Programming

R is a language for statistical computing and graphics. It employed for in-depth data analysis. It supplies a variety of evaluations.

## Characteristics

Data storage and management facility,

It provides a suite of operators for calculations on arrays, specifically, matrices.

It provides a coherent collection of data that is an excellent tool for information analysis.

It provides facilities for data analysis Screen either onscreen or onto hardcopy.

## 13. IBM SPSS Modeler

IBM SPSS Modeler is a large data analytics that is a predictive platform. It provides systems, groups, people, and the venture and gives models. It's a variety of evaluation methods and algorithms.

## Characteristics

Discover insights by assessing, and resolve problems structured and unstructured information

Use an interface for everyone to find out.

You can choose from cloud on-premises and setup that is hybrid choices.

Pick the algorithm according to version functionality.

## 8 Top Big Data Analytics Tools

Big Data is all about amassing large (or "Large") volumes of unstructured and structured information. Why is Big Data helpful is an investigation of the information to discover significance and patterns that could be left undiscovered. Making sense of Big Data is the domain of Big Data analytics applications, which offer price that is competitive to be derived by capacities for business.

We seem characteristics of the marketplace.

Zoho Analytics

Cloudera

Microsoft Power BI

Oracle Analytics Cloud

Pentaho Big Data Integration and Analytics

SAS Institute

Sisense

Splunk

Tableau

## What do you need to search for when choosing Big Data Analytics tools for your industry?

*Analytic Capabilities:* There are multiple kinds of analytics abilities with versions such as market basket analysis, decision trees, time series, neural networks, route analysis, predictive mining, and link analysis.

*Integration:* Often added tools and Programming languages (for instance, R) are required by the company to run different kinds of habit analysis.

*Data Export and Import:* Getting data in and out of tools is a crucial characteristic, and knowing how hard (or natural) it connects the analytics application into the vast information repository is a vital consideration.

*Visualization:* Seeing the amounts is one thing, but having Information displayed in a graphic format makes the information more usable.

*Scalability:* Big Data could be significant, to begin with, and has a propensity to grow larger over time. Comprehend, and organizations should think about the alternatives for the applications that they select.

*Collaboration:* Analysis can be a solitary exercise; however, often, it entails cooperation.

## Zoho Analytics emblem

Zoho Analytics is a self-service alternative that will not want the aid of information scientists or IT personnel to glean knowledge. The Zoho data applications have an intuitive drag and drop interface, in addition to an interface that is traditional.

Recognizing the varied data resources of today, Zoho Analytics lets link into a wide selection. Included in these are files saved in cloud pushes business applications as well as your company software. Following a question, results could look at in tabular views, graphs dashboards, and KPI visualizations.

In other words, the platform could access from the data experts in the C package to the sales reps who want info analytics trend lines. Zoho Analytics enables users to make a remark threat in the program to ease cooperation between groups and staffers. Zoho is a fantastic choice for companies that must provide data analytics insight into staffers.

## Cloudera

When it comes to the heart of Big Data, few are tied as Cloudera together with the Hadoop Big Data source platform that was open. After all, the creators of Hadoop itself began the provider. Cloudera got an even more significant foothold at the Hadoop ecosystem together with Hortonworks' merger that was its rival.

The main differentiator for Cloudera is your company's core and comprehension proficiency in Hadoop that communicates through its portfolio, such as the Cloudera Enterprise platform of the company. It can build on top of the source CDH distribution.

The Big Data tools of Cloudera are a fantastic match for organizations that needs a stack, which includes Hadoop technologies. Together with Cloudera Enterprise, organizations able to make procedure and analytics versions that are predictive, employing an assortment of applications that integrated

## Microsoft Power BI Microsoft

The Power BI of Microsoft was a favorite for analyst companies in the company intelligence area, predicated on the ease of availability and use of the platform.

In 2018, Power BI enlarged, extending the same simplicity to Big Data of usage, allowing transformation and data ingest. The primary differentiator for the system is integration using all the Azure Data

Lake Storage Gen2, which supports HDFS (Hadoop Distributed File System) for sophisticated, extensive data analytics.

Power BI is a fantastic choice for organizations to Big Data that can be pick and analytics. Power BI supplies cloud-based business analytics also incorporates what Microsoft calls "content packs" with pre-built dashboards and documents for several sorts of investigation and information monitoring. The collaboration capabilities in the system empower users to share dash and information, while also providing alerting capabilities.

## Oracle Analytics Cloud Oracle

Oracle has called a Big Data Analytics Provider, but it is a distance where the database giant has moved into in the past few decades. Data analytics on an intake usage model is precisely what the Oracle Analytics Cloud is related to.

One of the key differentiators of this Oracle Analytics Cloud that users remark on is the automation capabilities for various kinds of Data investigation use-cases along with analytics of your platform. Organizations that utilized Oracle tools, such as Oracle's namesake database, will be very drawn to the Analytics Cloud offering.

The ability to deliver multiple data sources is a core capacity using a reliable infrastructure which such as the Oracle Event Hub Cloud supports to ingest the Oracle Big Data Cloud Service as well as information to keep info.

# Hitachi VantaraPentaho Hitachi

Hitachi is not a title which many would associate Big Data; it's become a player in the area.

Pentaho's roots use its open-source analytics platform upon which the expansive enterprise variant constructed. It is the open-source nature of the system that has resulted in a community and is an integral differentiator.

Pentaho is a fantastic choice for organizations with a lot of kinds of signs and information data resources. The capability combines and to ingest data is another advantage that consumers gain from the Analytics stage and your Pentaho Big Data Integration. Pentaho's platform allows models such as analytics to assist organizations direct toward results.

## SAS Visual Analytics

SAS Institute has a long history in the market that predates using Big Data as a tech and a word. The business has domain experience in analytics that's manifest; one of them is across a lot of offerings that may help with Big Data Analytics.

Visual Analytics is for organizations and customers who are on the lookout together with drop and drag operation for constructing complex visualizations. Extensibility of this platform, for several kinds of information, coverage demands, and business intelligence is an integral differentiator for the stage.

Collaboration is the capability as well with a core element to share remarks and information across choices such as web browsers, web browsers, mobile devices as well as Microsoft Office programs. SAS Visual Analytics may be deployed on-premises or as support from the cloud.

## Sisense

Obtaining Big Data repositories at a country rapidly employed for analytics is a non-trivial challenge, which Sisense intends to help solve using its stage

The guarantee of helping make it more comfortable to get Big Data Prepared for analysis is a crucial differentiator for Sisense and a place of strength. They were using its Big Data planning skills that goal to create is more natural for consumers to simulate information.

Sisense is a fantastic option searching for customer care that is strong and quick implementation time. Consumers often see the information visualization through the system's dashboard as a time saver for the outcomes and as being simple to use. Sharing information and obtaining the panels is another power with net and cellular options in addition to the capability to generate various kinds of reports.

## Splunk

Splunk has discovered and started as a log evaluation platform, a loyal center of associations and consumers that adore how the platform visualizations and functions and empowers data manipulation. For those organizations which are currently utilizing other kinds of investigation or Splunk for log, embracing Splunk Analytics for Hadoop is a simple step.

As a stage, it is known for its internet Splunk Based log analytics and review. The system benefits from an established cooperation component and empowers users to produce and share analytics dashboards and charts.

Critical differentiators for Splunk contain the capability to incorporate with other elements such as safety, of this Splunk platform Controls and search procedure language (SPL), which further supplies advantages to users.

## Tableau

The Tableau platform is a pioneer in the analytics marketplace and is a fantastic alternative for scientists working across almost any industry, in businesses.

The Viz QL data visualization technologies in the center of Tableau are an integral differentiator for the stage generating data visualization without the need. Backends and kinds of Big Data is a core feature of this Tableau platform.

A benefit that consumers locate from Tableau is your ability to reuse abilities, at the Big Data context. Tableau uses a standardized SQL (Structured Query Language) to interface and query with Big Data systems, which makes it possible for businesses to use current database and analyst skills places to discover the insights they're searching for, by a massive data collection. Tableau also incorporates its in-memory data engine known as "Hyper," allowing fast information lookup and investigation.

## 8 Open Source Big Data Tools to utilize in 2018

Big Data analytics is a vital part of any company that is of the workflow. We advocate using these Big Data options to take advantage of it.

Opting for open source Big Data tools rather than for alternatives, you may ask? The reason became evident over the previous decade the program is the best way.

Developers choose to avoid vendor lock-in and tend to use free tools because of the option to donate to the evolvement of the platform. Open source products boast the same or even superior degree of instruction thickness, together with more active service from the neighborhood, that will also be the product programmers and Big Data professionals, who understand what they want out of a product. Said this is the list of 8 Big Data instrument that is sexy to utilize according to celebrity, characteristic richness, and endurance.

## 1. Apache Hadoop

The champion in the area of Big Data processing, famous for information because of its capacities. At or on-prem, the cloud cans operate and contains low hardware requirements. The primary Hadoop advantages and attributes will be as follows:

HDFS -- Hadoop Distributed File System, oriented at functioning together with huge-scale bandwidth

MapReduce -- a model that is configurable for Big Data processing

YARN -- a source scheduler for Hadoop resource management

Hadoop Libraries -- the glue for allowing third-party modules to operate with Hadoop

## 2. Apache Spark

Apache Spark is your alternative and, in some aspects, the Apache Hadoop's successor. Spark was built to tackle Hadoop's shortcomings even it does so well: it works with MapReduce and can process both batch info and real-time information thanks to data processing capacities.

Spark works along with cloud and on-prem, includes another tier of operations to your company, with Apache, OpenStack, and HDFS Cassandra.

## 3. Apache Storm

It is just another Apache product real-time frame. Storm scheduler works with Hadoop HDFS and balances the workload between nodes based on the setup. Apache Storm gets the following advantages:

Great horizontal scalability

Built-in fault-tolerance

Auto-restart on crashes

Clojure-written

Works together with Direct Acyclic Graph (DAG) topology

Output documents are in JSON format.

## 4. Apache Cassandra

Apache Cassandra is one of those columns supporting the enormous victory of Facebook, as it permits to process data collections spread throughout the world. It functions nicely under heavy workloads Because of Its structure with no single points of failure and boasts exceptional capabilities no additional NoSQL or relational DB has, for example:

Fantastic lining scalability

The simplicity of operations Because of a straightforward Question language used

Replication across nodes

Straightforward removal and adding of nodes from a running bunch

High fault tolerance

Built-in high availability

## 5. MongoDB

MongoDB is just another example of an open-source NoSQL database using features, which can be harmonious with numerous programming languages that are cross-platform. IT Svit utilizes MongoDB in many different tracking options and cloud computing, and we developed a module for MongoDB copies. The most prominent MongoDB attributes are:

Shops any kind of data and integer to strings, arrays, dates and boolean

Installation and high flexibility of configuration

Data partitioning across multiple nodes and data centers

As lively, cost savings Schemas allow information processing on the move

## 6. R Programming Environment

R used alongside the Jupiter pile (Julia, Python(R) for empowering wide-scale statistical analysis and information visualization. Jupiter laptop is among four popular Big Data visualization applications, as it permits composing any analytic model from over 9,000 CRAN (Comprehensive R Archive Network) modules and algorithms. They are running it in handy surroundings, correcting it on the head, and scrutinizing the analysis results simultaneously. The main advantages of using R would be as follows:

The SQL server can be operating within by R

R operates on Linux and Windows servers.

R supports Spark and Apache Hadoop.

R is mobile

R readily scales from one evaluation Machine to enormous Hadoop data ponds.

## 7. Neo4j

Neo4j is an open-source chart database in keeping information that follows the routine that is key-value. IT Svit has assembled an AWS infrastructure, and the database works under the heavy workload of requests and community information. Main Neo4j attributes are as follows:

Constructed support for transactions

Cipher chart query language

High-availability and scalability

Due to the lack of schemas

Integration with other databases

## 8. Apache SAMOA

It is just another of the Apache household of tools utilized for Big Data processing. Constructing spread streaming algorithms for Big Data exploration that is effective is specialized in by Samoa. This instrument is built with structure and must be utilized, such as Apache Storm, we said previously under Apache products. Its additional attributes used for Machine Learning comprise the following:

Clustering

Classification

Normalization

Regression

Programming primitives Customized algorithms

Using Apache Samoa empowers the Distributed stream processing engines to present these concrete advantages:

Use anywhere, program after

Reuse the Present infrastructure for new Jobs

No reboot or installation downtime

No need for copies or time-consuming Upgrades

## Final ideas among the listing of sexy Big Data tools for 2018

Big Data information science evolves, and business improved a significant deal recently and quickly found in 2017. It is only one of the IT styles together with ML, blockchain, AI &IoT, of 2018.

Big Data analytics is programs that are prevalent from using source Big Data, and ML to government and healthcare would be any Big Data builder's toolkit's mainframe if you happen to have any issues.

# CHAPTER 5

# PROGRAMMING METHODS

# WITH PYTHON AND C++

## What's the ideal programming language for Machine Learning?

There's much more action in machine learning more compared to occupation offers from the West can explain, and peer feedback areas such might confound the novices and valuable but frequently contradictory. We turned instead to our difficult information from 2,000+ info scientists and machine teaching programmers who responded to our most recent questionnaire about which languages they use and what jobs they are working.

Subsequently, we could not help but run several versions to determine which would be. We contrasted the top-5 languages, and the results show that there's not a straightforward reply to this "which speech?" question. It depends on what you are attempting to construct, what your background is, and why you got involved with the machine.

# Which system learning terminology has become the most popular complete?

First, let us look at the machine's prevalence learning languages. Python leads the bunch, with 33% prioritizing it and 57 percent of system learning programmers and information scientists utilizing it. The small wonder gave the development in the learning frameworks within the previous two decades, including a collection of libraries plus the launch of TensorFlow. Python often compared to R, but they're nowhere near equal concerning fame: R comes fourth in total use (31 percent) and fifth in prioritization (5 percent). R is the language using the cheapest ratio among the five, with just 17. It implies that R is a language, not an option.

The identical rate for Python is currently at 58%, the highest by far one of the five words. Not only is it Python the most commonly used language, but it's also the first selection for nearly all its consumers. C/C++ is a distant second to Python, both in use (44 percent) and prioritization (19 percent). Java follows C/C++ quite tightly, although JavaScript comes fifth in use, but with slightly higher prioritization functionality than R (7 percent). We asked our respondents about other languages used in machine learning, including the typical suspects of Julia, Scala, Ruby, Octave, MATLAB, and SAS. However, all of them fall under the 5 percent mark of prioritization and 26 percent of use. We focused our attention.

Python prioritized in software where Java isn't our data shows that the crucial element when selecting a language for machine learning is. In our survey, we asked programmers about 17 different program areas while also supplying our respondents with the chance to inform us they are still researching choices, not working on any place. Here we provide bottom and the best few places per speech: those where programmers prioritize every address the least and the most.

Machine learning scientists prioritize Python (44 percent) and R (11 percent) more and JavaScript (2 percent) and Java (15 percent) less than programmers working on different locations. Both regions and fraud detection, in contrast, is prioritized more by people's cyber-attacks. In which Java is a favorite of most improvement teams -- network security and fraud detection algorithms are constructed or absorbed in businesses -- and notably in institutions. In regions which are not as enterprise-focused, for example, natural language processing (NLP) and opinion analysis, programmers opt for Python that provides a more straightforward and quick way to construct highly performing calculations, because of the broad group of specialized libraries which include this.

Artificial Intelligence (AI) in matches (29 percent) and robot Locomotion (27 percent) are the two regions where C/C++ is well known the most, given the amount of management, higher performance, and efficiency demanded. Here a lower-level programming language like C/C++, which includes highly complex AI libraries, is a natural option, while R, made for statistical evaluation and visualizations, is mainly deemed insignificant. AI in games (3 percent) and robot locomotion (1 percent) are the two regions where R prioritized the least, followed by speech recognition at which the situation is comparable.

Apart from in opinion analysis, R is comparatively Highly prioritized -- as in comparison to other program areas -- in bioengineering and bioinformatics (11 percent), a place where both Java and JavaScript aren't favored—considering that the usage of R from data. Both inside and outside academia, it is not surprising that it is one of the regions. Ultimately, our data demonstrate that programmers new to information machine and science learning that are still researching options prioritize JavaScript over others (11 percent) and Java significantly less than many others (13 percent). All these are, in many cases, programmers that are currently experimenting with machine learning via using a machine learning API in a web application.

Professional wallpaper is critical in choosing a machine learning terminology. Secondly, the program area, Expert background is also critical in choosing a machine learning terminology. The programmers prioritizing the top-five languages higher than many others come from five distinct backgrounds. Python is prioritized the most by people for whom information science is the very first profession or discipline of research (38 percent). It implies that Python has become an essential component of information science -- it has developed to information scientists' language. The same can't state for R, that can be prioritized mainly by data analysts and statisticians (14 percent), since the word was initially created for these, substituting S.

Web developers extend their use of JavaScript to Machine learning, 16% prioritizing it for this purpose while remaining clear of this clumsy C/C++ (8 percent). In the precise contrary, stand embedded computing hardware/electronics engineers that proceed for C/C++ over many others while averting JavaScript, Java, and R over others. Considering in controlling C/C + + within their technology life their investment, it might make no sense to settle for a language that would compromise their degree of control. Embedded computing hardware engineers will also be the most likely to be focusing on near-the-hardware machine learning jobs, for example, IoT border analytics jobs, where hardware can force their language choice. Our data confirm that their participation is above average amongst others in robot locomotion jobs and care, image classification.

It's the application programmers who prioritize it over others (21 percent), which can be in line with its usage mostly in enterprise-focused software, as mentioned earlier. Enterprise developers tend to use Java, such as machine learning, in most endeavors. The business directive in this instance can be evident from the next aspect that's strongly correlated to terminology prioritization -- the motive to enter machine learning. Java is prioritized the maximum (27 percent) by programmers who got into machine learning since their boss or business requested them. It's the least favorite (14%) by people who got to the area simply as they were interested in finding out what all the fuss has been about -- Java isn't a language

84

which you generally learn just for fun! It's Python the curious prioritize more than many others (38 percent), yet another sign that Python recognized as the most important language that one wants to experiment to learn which machine learning is related.

It appears that information science taught by some university's courses must catch up with this idea. Programmers who say they got to machine learning since information science is/was a part of the college diploma would be the least inclined to prioritize Python (26 percent) and the most likely to one hundred (7 percent) compared to other people. There's still a favorable bias towards R in data circles in academia -- in which it created -- as information machine and science learning gravitate more towards calculating, the tendency is slowly fading away. People who have college training in data science might prefer it over others; however, in absolute terms, it is still only a tiny portion of the group also that will opt for R.

People who wish to Improve them prioritize more c/C + + Present apps/projects with machine learning (20 percent) and less by people who aspire to construct new highly aggressive programs based on machine learning (14 percent). These routine points to C/C++ mostly utilize in technology jobs and IoT or even AR/VR programs, probably already composed in C/C++, to which ML-supported performance has added. When constructing a new application from scratch -- particularly one using NLP to get chatbots -- there is no specific reason to utilize C/C++. At the same time, there are loads of reasons to go for languages offering highly specialized libraries, such as Python. These languages may more quickly and readily yield highly performing algorithms which may provide a competitive edge in new ML-centric apps.

There's not any such thing as the best terminology for system learning. Our information demonstrates that prevalence is not a great yardstick to use when choosing a programming language for information science and machine learning. There's not any such thing as a 'best language for machine learning,' and it all depends upon what you would like to construct, where you are coming from and that you got involved in machine learning. Typically, developers interface the terminology they were using into machine learning, mainly if they are supposed to use it in projects next to their past work -- for example, technology jobs for C/C++ programmers or internet visualizations for JavaScript programmers.

In case your first touch programming is Machine learning, your peers at our poll point to Python since the best alternative, given its abundance of libraries and simplicity of usage. Be well prepared to utilize Java if, on the other hand, if you are dreaming about a project in a business environment. In any situation, these are exciting times for machine learning, and the travel is sure to be a mind-boggling one, despite the terminology you go for it.

## Python vs. C++ for Machine Learning -- Language Replies

Machine learning is among the issues in software development for a good reason, and now. Machine learning opens an entire world of possibilities for exciting app owners, programmers, and end-users. From customization to brighter recommendations, enhanced search capabilities, smart assistants, and software that may view, listen and respond -- machine learning may enhance a program and the experience of using it in all manner of means.

Machine learning is a subset of artificial intelligence (AI) that provides computers with the ability to "learn" -- i.e., progressively enhance performance on a task -- from information without relying on rule-based programming. It's the tradition of utilizing algorithms to parse and learn from data, then automatically make a forecast or "figure out" how to execute a specific job.

OK -- but that programming language is your best when it comes to machine learning? If you have got a concept for a new job that will demand machine learning abilities, it is crucial that you make the ideal option, for your achievement (or failure) of your program will probably lapse upon it.

You'll require a language learning library. You need a community of developer's decent runtime performance tool support and a wholesome ecosystem of bundles.

There are many language boxes we are going to narrow down the field to two of their very popular -- C++ and Python. Let us find out how they compare and have a look.

## Popularity

As per a poll of machine and info scientists Learning programmers -- ran by Developer Economics -- Python is the machine. Fifty-seven percent of survey respondents used it, with 33% prioritizing it. C++ arrived second -- though only 19 percent were prioritizing the speech for machine learning advancement, it used by 44 percent. (Taking the next, fourth, and fifth places were Java, R, and JavaScript, respectively.)

Is Python popular than C++? A great deal of it comes down to the simple fact that Python is simple to use in training compared to C++ and is quite simple to learn. You do not need a lot of software engineering expertise to begin using Python, and it has several libraries prepared to work for the functions of information analysis and machine learning. Additionally, academics have implemented their versions meaning versions printed in newspapers are accessible in the kind of implementations in Python.

Jupyter Notebooks have been instrumental in assisting student programmers in learning how to use Python for study, machine learning, and information science. Jupyter intended for Julia, Python, and R (thus the title -- it had previously called IPython), is also an open-source internet application, which enables users to create and share files, which feature live code, equations, visualizations, along with the explanatory text. Jupyter Notebooks are textbooks, filled with illustrations and explanations that students may try out in their browsers.

There Are Lots of additional services Laptops like google lab, also -- Google cloud hosting support for AI programmers, which has access. Google Colab ties in with Google Drive, Laptops, and meaning datasets can save there. There's nothing else out there using a lower cost of entry, which has helped as the system with Python's fame.

## Performance

There are a couple of places where C++ outperforms Python.

For Starters, C++ gets the benefit of being a statically typed language, which means that you won't have kind errors appear during runtime. The functionality crown goes to C++, as C++ generates runtime and a more streamlined code. There are techniques to optimize the system so that it runs. By way of instance, there are optimizing extensions for Python, for example, Cython, which can be Python with static typing -- because Cython statically typed, it is simple to compile it into C/C++ and then operate in C/C++ rates. Thus, there's no difference.

That Python is a dynamic (rather than static) Language has some benefits of its own not because it optimizes programmer efficiency and reduces complexity regarding collaborating, and that means that you may execute with less code. In which all compilers can be stage-specific and tend to perform optimization, Python code may run on any platform that is just about without wasting time on configurations.

Another factor is the growth of GPU-accelerated computing. GPUs have contributed to abilities for parallelism production like cuDNN and CUDA Python. Now machine learning workloads have offloaded into GPU advantage that C++ might have is becoming more and more irrelevant.

## Simplicity and Usability

Python is famous for its easily readable and shortcode, making its high esteem for simplicity and the ease-of-use -- especially. The same can't state for C++, which is regarded as a lower-level language, meaning it is a lot easier to read to your pc (hence its higher performance), although harder to read for people.

Python syntax allows for a more natural and intuitive ETL (Extract, Transform, and Load) process, which also means it is quicker for advancement compared to C++, enabling programmers to test machine learning algorithms without needing to apply them rapidly.

For us, the winner for the system between C++ and Python learning is Python. There is a reason it is so popular -- using its simple syntax and readability encouraging the fast testing of complicated machine learning algorithms. A booming community strengthened by collaborative tools like Jupyter Notebooks and Google Collab, and a broad choice of machine-learning-specific libraries to boot up; Python has everything.

Therefore, if you are organizing a job that is new with Machine learning abilities and wish to understand whether C++, Python, or some other language are the most suitable, get in contact with Netguru. We are going to chat through your needs and advise you on the best route ahead.

## Top ten programming Methods

There has been lots of disagreement about which programming; finally, it does not matter; however, language is most suitable for teaching students to plan. Learning to program is not about syntax; it is all about the thinking. It is not all about learning the orders out of Codecademy; it is also about breaking down a task into several measures. That is why I don't like the expression "programming" - it is not exactly what we are attempting to educate.

Scientists inform us that we recall and understand the things we believe. We will need to be sure our courses get pupils to consider what we want them to understand. That is why word searches don't have any educational value (besides for instructing pupils to spell); they make pupils consider precisely what the words seem, as opposed to what they imply.

I wouldn't start students off assessing syntax errors in code. It isn't so exciting, and it appears -- such as getting kids to books. More crucially, it is getting pupils to consider the not-very-important problem of syntax (they can perform if they want to) if they need to be considering the programming methods and the actions necessary to make the program.

With that in mind, I will inform you programming methods that are language-independent will operate in almost any language. I believe they form a fantastic foundation for a KS3 programming class. You may add illustrations in your selected language to exemplify the thoughts, and perhaps use the list as a checklist of things to test if approaching a new programming endeavor.

A listing of techniques will contain a belief that there is a need to expand on a few of the thoughts in future

## 1. Factors

You are unlikely to have the ability to create an exciting or useful program that does not store any info - you would not wish to play with a game that could not give a rating to you. Factors are the essential thing in programming. The number of forms, and if you have to announce them changes from language to language, that explains the reason why I begin with just fundamental (with two different types -- strings and numbers) and progress into Visual Basic (with more forms, but the very same controls).

## 2. Repetition/Loops

I believe that loops are, although not arranged, perhaps it is the most significant construct in programming.

Undoubtedly, the most frequent type of reproduction within my Programs, though I discover that self-taught students usually are obsessed with utilizing while for all - I am not sure why, as in many instances, it generates a more sophisticated solution. In nearly all languages, it utilizes the concept of counting. However, in Python, it iterates through a list or series, also in JavaScript, it may use to loop through a "set" of items on a webpage in a similar manner.

## 3. Decisions/Selection

Wouldn't be engaging or elastic, so we will need to receive our programs to respond to occasions and user input. In addition to this almost universal, if then else construct, many programming languages (but not Python) have case/preferred way of controlling program flow. You might even utilize array/list indicators as a kind of choice (see below).

## 4. Arrays

Arrays are useful for groups of like things, e.g., lottery chunks, but using indicators as a kind of look-up or choice is a helpful technique. By way of instance, we could only create arbitrary numbers, so if we need a random item, like a day of this week, we could utilize the random number as the index within a range of strings containing the names of these times.

Python does not have support for arrays. However, several of their performance can reproduce using tuples or lists. Sparsely populated collections, or implementing a binary tree in a variety, can be somewhat cluttered, but as are two-dimensional arrays.

I am a big fan of JavaScript, but that does not encourage multi-dimensional arrays. What JavaScript does let, however, which may be helpful, is getting true and untrue as the selection index -- I used that procedure in my binary page. It usually means that you will use an expression that evaluates as true or false as an indicator, creating a kind of choice.

## 5. Boolean Logic

Pupils will need to know about AND, OR, NOT, etc., blending truth values, and making precision tables; however, boolean operators are used each time in programming.

An important matter for students is that expressions (e.g., equalities or inequalities) assess as true or untrue, so if, by way of instance, always functions on false or true. It follows that we can use syntax like if x instead of if x == accurate, but also that expressions like x + 10 == 20 or x% five> 0 will evaluate as either true or false and may even utilize as array indexes in languages like JavaScript.

## 6. Bitwise Logic

Using logic to hide and set/unset bits was something of a programming staple once when I was a teen, and memory was at a top. It might use to combine multiple values also to hide pieces to conserve memory and to examine them.

Dijkstra called (in 1979) that "the arrival of cheap and strong devices will place personal science back 25 years". The requirement to conserve memory has mostly passed, but that remains a helpful method for combining many values to maneuver between functions as one argument, or to give varying quantities of costs involving webpages in a cookie-cutter or query string. It is also possible to utilize it like a fast and easy means to convert between denary and binary options or to encipher text such as a Lorenz machine with bitwise EOR.

## 7. Modular Arithmetic

It is the subject of a site. However, Arithmetic is currently breaking up and looking at the rest. It is a fantastic method of restricting the number of outputs of an app or purpose or of having things to "wrap-around," e.g., getting angles to move from 359 back to 0. It is so straightforward and so useful that a method that I can't think why you would not include it in almost any KS3 programming program.

## 8. Manipulating Text

I have alienated here by combining the handling of strings and characters. They are different items, but I needed to slip at number ten into trigonometry!

Having the capability to convert characters to ASCII and vice versa is a helpful method for many different reasons. You may use it to look for upper/lower case, as an instance, or non-alphabetic personalities, and you could also use ASCII codes to make Caesar change ciphers or Lorenz-style ciphers using bitwise EOR.

## 9. Random Numbers and Scaling

Many languages, such as Python, have library purposes of creating arbitrary integers (i.e., ran dint ()). Still, you may use a word that does not, or you may not need to have an integer, so it is beneficial to understand how to scale arbitrary numbers yourself. Mounting amounts usually -- e.g., for matching items onto a screen -- is a useful skill. I demonstrate this technique in my polygon program to make sure that the polygon is always the same size, whatever the number of sides.

You may want a random number for its own sake, e.g., to simulate a die roll to utilize as an array/list indicator to decide on a random item. But it is also possible to add a level of randomness to details to make them seem more "organic." I used recursion to create a tree scratch, but it did not resemble a tree. An outcome is created by adding a little bit of randomness.

Python's ran dint () function along with the scaling process I explain pseudorandom numbers, which uniformly dispersed throughout the range that is selected. You may not want this to be the situation. By way of instance, on my page, I wanted angles to select more frequently since corners which pupils encounter are significantly less than 180º.

The answer is easy; since the operation in many languages creates a number between 1 and 0, if you increase that amount to some power, it remains between 1 and 0, but the supply varies. Should you square the amount, by way of instance, 0 remains as 0 1 remain 1. However, 0.5 becomes 0.25 -- i.e., the distribution is skewed towards the lower amounts. You must do that just subtract the result if you would like to skew the supply upward.

# 10. Trigonometry

I went with "Maths" with this last stage, because understanding mechanisms issues, like Newton's equations of motion or conservation of momentum, may be helpful if creating animation or games. "Maths" could be somewhat broad, however, so I have selected trigonometry since, though I do not use it daily, it's the advanced mathematical technique I use frequently.

Sines and cosines are helpful when drawing circles, making the motion, and laying out things on a webpage, making patterns for exercising the angles of lines and direction. They may utilize in discussions of programming efficacy since the functions are very complex.

You may disagree with some inside my listing, or you may have others that you would need to include (procedures and functions are essential, as an instance, but I did not add them since you want to have some methods to use in these functions and processes). So why don't you join us at the TES Community to debate the subject (or make a ribbon in your forum of decision)?

# C++ Advanced: Extended Programming Techniques for C++ Developers

Given the increase in software, sophistication applications benefit from constructs; added support is offered extensions and by modifications of their standard.

Intro

C++ background

Standard compiler performance

Practical hints: Useful online links

## C++ Basics - Brief Summary

Keywords

Variable class's alignment

Classes and objects

Kinds that are constructor and destructor

Operators with overload

Function pointers in courses

Strings and flows

Class connections (institution, self-association, aggregation, Article, inheritance, multiple inheritance, and options)

## Interface concept with functions

Exercise: Comprehending the SW structure that is specified, you get to be aware of the builder layout, execute classes, composition, inheritance, and examine them mechanically using the TDD procedure (test-driven development).

You think about quality facets Programming, modularization, reusability, and extendibility.

# Exceptions

Exception handling - programming and definition

Exception classes and hierarchies

User exceptions

C++ standard exceptions

Hints: tips and Concepts

Exercise: Adding exception handling from the Exercise program

# Runtime Type Identification (IRTTI)

RTTI - programming and definition

Type info course

Relation to exception handling

Software and effects in usage

# New Style Casts

Dynamic, static, const and reinterpret cast

The choice for use

Relation to exception handling and RTTI

# Performance Control

Memory sections (BSS block started by symbol, pile, pile)

Comparison and evaluation of data segments

Dynamic memory management with delete and new

Overload (local and international) of brand new and delete

Algorithms

Virtual destructor

Placement new

Relation to exception handling

Bright pointers (also from the STL)

Hints: preventing pitfalls and Identifying risks

Template Functions and Template Courses

Standard performance

Template functions classes and their program

Cases of classes that are template

Inheritance and interfaces together with classes

Assembler, optimization and runtime and memory evaluation

Containers in STL style

Runtime time polymorphism

Perfect forwarding with templates

Template functions and classes

Alias templates

Illustrations for classes that are template

Exercise: Implementing the observer pattern Program and implementing it according to a personal, container-type template course

## STL Standard Template Library

Container adapters, containers

Iterators

Function items, algorithms

Memory allocator course

Suggestion: Overview of STL container components and Their relationship

Exercise: Implementing the observer pattern Program and implementing it based in an STL container course

## Multithreading and Atomic Data types

Multithreading - fundamental concepts

A prospective, threads condition variable

Implementing the mechanics

Practice: Adapting the program to a timer and Controlling it employing a system that is operating that is an extra abstraction with wrapper classes

Regular Expression

Functionality and program

regex library

Practical examples

## Performance

Facets and consumption behavior: program, info Memory and CPU processing time

Overhead minimization and functionality maximization

Checklist - evaluation of the Major language constructs

Practical suggestion compilers

## Average Pitfalls and Popular Idioms (PIMPL, RAII, NVI)

RAII (resource acquisition is initialization), source wrapper

NVI (non-virtual ports)

PIMPL (pointer to execution)

Managing

Practical hints idioms

## Exercises at the C++ Advanced Coaching

You may use it for executing the Microsoft Visual Studio Whole exercise (watch program).

## Micro Consult Plus:

All participants have the following choices to utilize Their exercises as well as the solutions created by Micro Consult in this workshop:

You simply take the documents with you on a free rod

MicroConsult, or.

You email the documents to your accounts, or.

You get access to file download request.

You receive the UML version of this watch as well as the C++ app code application.

You get all illustrations and can fix them.

You receive a beneficial notation summary for UML (Unified Modeling Language) in the DIN-A3 format.

# Beginner Strategies for Learning Python Programming

We are excited that you Have Opted to embark on studying Python journey! Among the most frequent questions we get from our subscribers is, "What is the perfect way to learn Python?"

I think the very first step in studying any programming Language is currently making sure you know how to understand. Learning is a skill.

Is expressive to find out valuable? The Solution is Easy: libraries have made, and resources are updated, as languages evolve. Understanding how to learn will be crucial to getting a programmer and keeping up with such changes.

## Make It Stick

Here are a few tips to assist you in creating the concepts learning as a novice developer stick:

Hint #1: Code every day

Consistency is essential once you are studying a new language. We advocate making a dedication. It might be challenging to think, but muscular memory plays with a role in programming. A regular commitment to coding will help develop that muscle memory. Even though it can seem daunting initially, look at starting small with 25 minutes daily and working your way up out there.

Hint #2: Write It Out

You will, as you progress as a developer, wonder if you ought to be taking notes. Yes, you need to! Research indicates that taking notes is the most helpful for long-term retention. It will be particularly beneficial for people working towards the objective of being a full-time programmer, as most interviews will probably involve writing code on a whiteboard.

As soon as you start working on applications and projects, writing by hand may help you plan your code until you proceed into the pc. You may save yourself a great deal of time if you compose which works and courses you'll need, in addition to the way they could interact.

Hint #3: Go Interactive!

Whether you're learning about Python data structures (strings, lists, dictionaries, etc.) for your very first time or you're launching a program, the more interactive Python shell is going to be among the very best learning tools. We use it much on this website too!

To utilize the interactive Python shell (also sometimes known as a "Python REPL"), first ensure Python installed onto your PC. We have obtained a tutorial that will assist you in doing so. To trigger the interactive Python shell, and then just open your terminal and then run python or python3 based upon your setup. Directions can be found by you here.

Now You Know how to start the shell, then here are a few examples of how it is possible to use the shell when you're studying:

Discover what operations can perform within a component by using dir. ():

>>>my_string = 'I am a string'

>>>dir(my_string)

['__include __','upper', 'fill'] # Truncated for readability

The components returned from dir. () are all the methods (i.e., activities) which you can apply to this component. For instance:

>>>my_string.upper ()

>>> 'I AM A STRING.'

Notice that we predicted the top () method. Would you see what it does? It makes the letters in the string uppercase all! Find out more about these built-in techniques beneath "Manipulating strings" within this tutorial.

Discover an element's Kind:

```
>>>Kind (my_string)

>>>str
```

Utilize the aid system to get Whole documentation:

```
>>>help (str)
```

Publish libraries and play together:

```
>>>FromDateTime import DateTime

>>>dir(datetime)

['__include __','weekday', 'year'] # Truncated for readability

>>>datetime.now ()

datetime. datetime (2018, 3, 14, 23, 44, 50, 851904)
```

Shell commands:

```
>>> import os

>>>So. System ('ls')

python_hw1.py python_hw2.py README.txt
```

Hint #4: Take Breaks

It's important to step away, and when you're studying, absorb the concepts. The Pomodoro Technique will help you have a break, operate for 25 minutes, repeat the procedure, and used it. Taking breaks is essential to getting a successful study session when you're currently taking in a lot of details.

Breaks are essential once you're currently debugging. If you can't figure out exactly what's going wrong, have a rest and hit a bug. Step away from the computer, go for a stroll, or talk with a buddy.

In programming, the code should follow the principles of logic, and language will split everything. Eyes make a difference.

Hint #5: Develop a Bug Bounty Hunter

As soon as you begin, it is certain writing programs that are complex; you will encounter bugs in your code. It happens to most of us! Do not let you frustrate.

When It's essential to have a methodological where things are breaking approach that will assist you to discover, ensuring, and moving in the sequence in every component works is a means to get this done.

As soon as you have a notion of where things may be breaking down, add the following line of code in your script import PDB; PDB.set_trace () and execute it. Here is the Python debugger that will drop you in interactive mode. The debugger may also run from the command line with python -m PDB.

Make It Collaborative

Reevaluate your learning after things begin to stick with collaboration. Below are a few strategies.

Hint #6

Though coding might seem like a solitary task, it works best once you work. Once you're learning to code which you surround yourself with men and women that are learning well, It's essential. It will let you share.

If you do not understand anybody, do not be worried. There are lots of methods to meet with! Locate meetups or events or combine a learning community for fans, Pythonista Cafe!

## Hint Educate

It states that the best way is to educate it. Once you're learning Python, this is true. There are several methods to perform so: whiteboarding with other Python fans, composing blog articles describing newly acquired concepts, recording videos where you describe something you heard, or just talking to yourself on your PC. Each one of these strategies exposes any gaps besides will solidify your understanding.

## Hint Pair Program

Pair programming is working on finishing a job. Both programmers change between being the "driver" and the "navigator." The "driver" writes the code, while the "navigator" helps direct the problem solving and reviews the system as it's written. Switch to have the advantage of either side.

Pair programming has many advantages not merely have someone review your code, but also to see how someone may be considering an issue. Being vulnerable to thoughts and ways of thinking will assist you in the problem.

# Hint #9: Request "GOOD" Questions

People say there isn't any such thing as a harmful matter; nevertheless, regarding programming, it's likely to ask a question. When you're asking for assistance from somebody who has little or no circumstance on the issue you're trying to resolve, it's better to inquire fantastic queries by following this ritual:

G: Circumstance to what you're currently attempting to do describing the issue.

O: Summarize the issue.

O: your very best guess about what the issue may be. It enables the individual who's helping you not just to understand what you're thinking, but also understand you've done some thinking by yourself.

D: Demo that what's currently occurring. Contain a traceback, the code Error message, and an explanation of the measures. The individual doesn't need to attempt and recreate the matter.

Questions can save you a good deal of time. Skipping some of the measures could result. As a newcomer, you need to be sure to ask great questions, so you practice communication your idea process so that those who help you'll be delighted to keep on helping you.

## Make Something

Most, if not all, Developers you ask to will tell by doing you that to learn Python, you must learn. Exercises that are doing may only take you so much: you understand the most.

## Tip #10: Anything, Construct Something

There are help you create the muscle memory we talked about above, besides, to become convinced with Python. As soon as you've got a good grasp of fundamental data structures (strings, lists, dictionaries, sets), object-oriented programming, and writing courses, it is time to begin building!

Everything you construct isn't quite as crucial as you build it. The Travel of construction is what's going to teach the maximum to you. You can learn a lot from studying classes and Python articles. Most of your learning will come from using Python to construct something. The issues will teach a good deal to you.

There are many lists on the market with thoughts for newcomer Python jobs. Here are some suggestions to get you started:

Number guessing game

Simple calculator program

Dice roll simulator

Bitcoin Price Notification Service

Should you find it hard to think of a clinic that is Python jobs see this movie. It sets out you are feeling stuck a plan you can use to create thousands of job ideas.

Tip #11: Contribute to Open Source

From the open-minded version, application source code is available for everyone. There are lots of libraries which take gifts and are easy projects—furthermore, plans published by many businesses. Therefore, you may work with code made and written by the engineers.

Adding to a Python job is an excellent way to create learning experiences. Let's say you opt to submit a bug fix ask you to submit a "pull petition" to your repair to patch to the code.

The project supervisors will review your job remarks and suggestions. It will let you learn the practice, in addition to best practices for programming that is Python.

# CHAPTER 6

# MACHINE LEARNING ALGORITHMS

## Machine Learning Algorithms: What's a Machine Learning Algorithm?

Machine Learning algorithm is an evolution of the routine algorithm. It makes your apps "smarter" by enabling them to learn from the information you supply automatically. The plan mainly split into:

## Testing period

Building on the case, I'd given some time ago talk a bit about these phases.

## Training Stage

You require a randomly chosen specimen of apples in the Marketplace (training data). Create a table of all of the physical features of each vegetable, such as color, size, form, increased in which portion of the nation, offered by which seller, etc. (attributes ), alongside the sweetness, juiciness, ripeness of the apple (output factors ). You feed this information to the machine learning algorithm (classification/regression), and it learns a version of the correlation involving a mean apple's physical traits, and it is quality.

## Testing Period

Next time when you go shopping, you may quantify the features of the apples that you're buying (test data) and feed into the Machine Learning algorithm. It'll use the version that computed whether the apples are juicy, to forecast. The algorithm may internally use the principles, very similar to the one that you manually composed earlier (such as, e.g., a decision tree). Without worrying about the specifics of how to select the best apples, last, now you can search with assurance.

You know everything! You able to produce time improve over (reinforcement learning), so it will enhance its precision as it has trained on an increasing number of the training dataset; if it makes a prediction, it will upgrade its rule.

The best aspect of this can be, the algorithm can be used by you to train models that are different. You can make one each for calling the quality of bananas, mangoes, grapes, or whatever fruit you desire.

To get a detailed explanation on Machine Learning Algorithms, don't hesitate to go through this movie:

Let us categorize Machine Learning Algorithm to subparts and see precisely every one of these is employed in actual life, and what they each are, how they operate.

# Machine Learning Algorithms: What are the types of Machine Learning Algorithms?

Thus, the can categorizes Machine Learning Algorithms Following three different types.

Classification of Machine Learning - Machine Learning Algorithms

## Machine Learning Algorithms: What's Supervised Learning?

This class is known as learning the procedure for an algorithm that could be considered as a teacher. The effect continuously predicted by the algorithm and adjusted by the instructor. Before the algorithm achieves an acceptable level of functionality, the learning continues.

In each case of, supervised machine learning algorithm, the training dataset includes input characteristics and output that anticipated. The training dataset may take an audio frequency histogram, the pixels of a picture, or any type of information as input, like the worth of a database row.

Example: In Biometric Attendance, the device can be trained by you with inputs of your identity. It may become your thumb, iris or earlobe, etc. When the system trained, your information can be validated by it, and you can be indeed identified by and.

# Machine Learning Algorithms: What's Unsupervised Learning?

This kind of machine learning is so-called because there's not any teacher unsupervised. Reunion and algorithms are left to detect the structure from the data.

The target for learning is to mimic the structure or supply in the information to be able to find out more.

From the sample of a, the learning strategy training dataset doesn't have an output. Employing the learning algorithms patterns can be detected by you dependent on the features of the input information. Clustering can be an illustration of a machine learning task that employs the learning strategy. The machine sets data to identify clusters and samples.

Instance: Fraud Detection is most likely the most common use-case of unsupervised learning. It's likely to isolate claims based on its proximity to clusters that suggest fraudulent patterns.

# Machine Learning Algorithms: What's Reinforcement Learning?

Learning can think of just like a and trial process of studying. The machine has a penalty or reward stage for every action it functions. The device receives a penalty point or increases the reward stage if the alternative is right.

The reinforcement learning algorithm is about the interaction between the learning representative and the environment. The learning agent relies on manipulation and exploration.

Exploration is when trial and is acted on by the learning broker exploitation and mistake is as it performs an action based on the knowledge. The surroundings reward the agent. With the intent of amassing rewards, its surroundings knowledge enhances carry out or to select the work.

Let see how Pavlov trained his pet using reinforcement instruction?

Phase 1 Pavlov gave the dog meat. In reaction to this meat, the puppy began salivating.

Phase 2: At another stage, he created a sound using a bell. However, this time the puppies didn't respond to whatever.

Stage 3: At the next phase, he strove to train his dog by employing the bell and giving food to them and seeing the food that the dog began salivating.

The dogs began salivating after hearing the bell, as the puppy fortified that the alarm would ring even when food not given. He'll find the food. Reinforcement Learning is a process, either by opinions or stimulation.

# Machine Learning Algorithms: List of Machine Learning Algorithms

Here's the list of 5 machine learning algorithms.

· Linear Regression

· Logistic Regression

· Decision Tree

· Naive Bayes

· kNN

## Linear Regression

It uses to gauge actual values (the price of homes, number of calls (total earnings heat.) based on continuous variables. We establish a connection between the variables by matching the ideal line. This best match is popularly referred to as the regression line and symbolized with means of a linear equation $Y = aX + b$.

The best way to comprehend regression would be to relive this adventure of youth. Let's suppose; you ask people to be arranged by a young child in grade in his course by order of weight! What do you feel the kid is going to do? He/she would probably look (visually examine) in the peak and build of individuals and organize them with a blend of those parameters that are observable. It is a regression in actual life! The kid construct would be connected to the burden and has figured out the height.

In this equation:

Y -- Dependent Variable

a -- Slope

X -- Independent variable

b -- Intercept

Linear Regression - Machine Learning Algorithms - Edureka

All these and b are derived based on diminishing that the sum of squared differences of space between the regression line and data points.

Have a look at the plot. Here, we've identified the best match using linear equation y=0.2811x+13.9. Applying this equation, we could get the burden, realizing a person's height.

R-Code:

Train and datasets

#identify attribute and response factor (s) and worth must be numerical and NumPy arrays

```
x_train<- input_variables_values_training_datasets

y_train<- target_variables_values_training_datasets

x_test<- input_variables_values_test_datasets

X <- cbind (x_train, y train)

# Train the version assess score and places
```

```
Linear <- lm (y_train ~. data = x)

Outline (linear)

#Predict Output

Predicted = forecast (linear,x_test)
```

## Logistic Regression

Do not get confused by its title! It is a classification and not a regression algorithm. It's utilized to estimate discrete values (Binary values such as 0/1, yes/no, true/false) based on a particular set of the independent variable(s). It forecasts that the likelihood of the occurrence of an event by matching data into a function that is logit. It is called the logit regression. As it forecasts the chance, its output signal values lie between 1 and 0.

Let us understand and try this via an easy example.

Let us say your friend offers you a puzzle to solve. You will find only two result situations -- you resolve it, or you do not. Imagine you have a selection of puzzles/quizzes to understand which subjects you are good at. The study's results could be something similar to this -- you're 70% to solve it if you been provided a trigonometry based tenth-grade problem. If it is a standard fifth background query, the probability of receiving an answer is 30% that is exactly what Logistic Regression provides you.

Coming to the math, the log odds of this outcome is modeled as a linear combination of these predictor variables.

Likelihood = p/ (1-p) = probability of event occurrence / probability of not event occurrence ln(odds) = ln (p/ (1-p)) logit(p) = ln(p/(1-p)) = b0+b1X1+b2X2+b3X3...+bkXk

Above, p is the probability of the existence of this feature of interest. It selects parameters that maximize the probability of detecting the sample values rather than that decrease the sum of squared errors (such as in normal regression).

Why choose a log? You might ask. For the sake of simplicity, let's just say this is only one of the mathematical strategies to replicate a step function.

R-Code:

```
X <- cbind(x_train,y_train)
# Train the version using the training sets and assess score
Logistic <- glm(y_train ~ . , data = x,family='binomial')
Outline (logistic)
#Predict Output
Predicted = forecast (logistic,x_test)
```

Different steps could be approached to enhance the model:

Including interaction terms

Removing features

Regularization methods

# Employing a non-linear model

Decision Tree

Here is a kind of a supervised learning algorithm mostly used for classification problems. It works for both continuous and categorical variables. In this algorithm, we now divide the population into two or more homogeneous sets. It can be done in line with the most critical characteristics / independent factors to create as different groups as you can.

From the picture above, it is possible to see that the population is classified into four categories based on multiple characteristics to identify 'if they are going to play or not.'

R-Code:

Library (part)

X ‹- cbind(x_train,y_train)

# develop tree

fit<- rpart(y_train ~. , data = x,method="class")

Summary (fit)

#Predict Output

Predicted = predict (fit,x_test)

# Naive Bayes

It is a classification technique based on Bayes' theorem having an assumption of independence between predictors. A Naive Bayes classifier assumes the existence of a specific characteristic in a course is irrelevant to the existence of any additional attribute.

As an example, the fruit could be considered as an apple if it is reddish, round, and approximately 3 inches in diameter. Even though these attributes rely upon each other or on the presence of the other characteristics, a naive Bayes classifier would consider each one these properties to promote the probability that this fruit is an apple independently.

Naive Bayesian model is easy to construct and especially helpful for very large data sets. Together with simplicity, Naive Bayes has proven to outperform highly complex classification procedures.

Bayes theorem provides a method of calculating posterior probability $P(c|x)$ from $P(c)$, $P(x)$, and $P(x|c)$. Consider the equation below:

Bayes Rule - Machine Learning Algorithms - EdurekaHere,

$P(c|x)$ is the posterior probability of class (goal) given Predictor (feature).

$P(c)$ is the prior probability, of course.

$P(x|c)$ is the likelihood that's the probability of the Predictor given course.

P(x) is the prior probability of predictor.

Example: Let us know it with an example. Here I have a training data set of corresponding and weather target factor 'Play.' Now, we have to classify whether gamers will play or not predicated on weather conditions. Let us follow the below steps to do it.

## Step 1: Combine the data sets to the frequency table

Step 2: Produce a likelihood table by discovering the probabilities such as Overcast odds = 0.29, and the likelihood of playing is 0.64.

Naive Bayes - Machine Learning Algorithms - EdurekaStep 3: Now, use the Naive Bayesian equation to compute the posterior probability for each class. The class with the greatest posterior probability is the result of the prediction.

Problem: If the weather remains shining, is this statement is accurate?

We can solve it using the above-discussed method, therefore P(Yes | Sunny) = P(Sunny | Yes) * P(Yes) / P (Sunny)

Here we have P (Sunny |Yes) = 3/9 = 0.33, P(Sunny) = 5/14 = 0.36, P(Yes)= 9/14 = 0.64

## Course Curriculum

Data Science Certification Course using R

Weekday / Weekend Batches

Today, P (Yes | Sunny) = 0.33 * 0.64 / / 0.36 = 0.60, that has higher probability.

Naive Bayes uses a way to predict the probability of class based on various attributes. This algorithm is utilized in text classification as well as problems having multiple courses.

R-Code:

```
Library (e1071)

X <- cbind(x_train,y_train)

# Fitting model

Fit <-naiveBayes(y_train ~. , data = x)

Summary (fit)

#Predict Output

Predicted = predict (fit,x_test)
```

CNN (k- Nearest Neighbors)

It may use for regression and classification problems. It is use in classification issues in the business. K nearest neighbors is a very simple algorithm that classifies new cases and stores all cases by the majority of its K neighbors. The situation is frequent amongst its K nearest neighbors.

These distance functions maybe Manhattan, Euclidean, Hamming, and Murkowski space. The first three acts are used for constant function and the fourth person (Hamming) for categorical factors. If K = 1, then the case is assigned to its closest neighbor's course. Sometimes, picking K turns out to be a struggle while performing KNN modeling.

KNN - Machine Learning Algorithms

KNN can be mapped to our lives. If you would like to learn about someone, to gain access, and you may love to discover about his buddies!

R-Code:

Library (kNN)

X - cbind(x_train,y_train)

# Fitting model

Fit -knn(y_train ~. , data = x,k=5)

Summary (fit)

#Predict Output

Predicted = predict (fit,x_test)

Things to consider before choosing KNN:

## KNN is costly

Factors must be normalized else high range factors that can prejudice it

Works on pre-processing phase before going to KNN, for example, an outlier, sound removal

The 10 Greatest Machine Learning Algorithms for Data Science Beginners

In studying system learning interest has skyrocketed in the years because Harvard Business Review article called 'Data Scientist' that the 'most sexy task of this century.' But if you are just beginning in machine learning, then it may be a little hard to split. That's why we're assessing our article about machine learning algorithms for a beginner.

If you have got some expertise in machine and data science learning, you might be more interested in this in-depth tutorial about doing machine learning Python using sci-kit-learn, or within our system learning classes, which begin here. If you are not clear yet about the difference between "data science" and "machine learning," this report provides a fantastic explanation: machine learning and data science -- what makes them different?

## Kinds of Machine Learning Algorithms

There are three kinds of machine learning (ML)Algorithms:

Supervised Learning Algorithms:

Learning utilizes the mapping function, which turns input factors (X) to the output (Y). To put it differently, it solves for f in another equation:

$Y = f(X)$

It enables outputs when given new inputs.

We'll discuss two kinds of learning: classification and regression.

Classification can use to forecast the outcome of a sample when the output is in the kind of categories. A classification version may take a look at the input data and attempt to predict tags such as "ill" or even "healthy."

Regression can use to forecast the outcome of a given sample when the output factor is in the shape of real worth. As an instance, a regression model may process input information to forecast the amount of rainfall, the height of an individual, etc.

The five algorithms which we cover in this site -- Linear Regression, Logistic Regression, CART, Naïve-Bayes, and K-Nearest Neighbors (KNN) -- are cases of supervised learning.

Ensembling is another sort of learning. It means combining the prediction of multiple system learning models' which are weak to create a more accurate prediction on a sample. Algorithms 9 and 10 of the article -- Bagging bettering with XGBoost -- are examples of ensemble methods.

## Unsupervised Learning Algorithms:

When we have the learning versions are used when we only have input factors (X) and no corresponding output factors. They utilize unlabeled training data to simulate their data's structure.

## We will talk around three kinds of unsupervised learning:

Association is employed to detect the probability of this Co-occurrence in a set of things. Market basket evaluation uses it. By way of instance, an institution model may be used to discover that when a client purchases the bread, s/he is 80% likely also to purchase eggs.

Clustering can be used to set samples that items within the same cluster are like each other compared to the items from the other bunch.

Dimensionality Reduction is utilized to decrease the amount variable of a data set while ensuring that important information is still conveyed. Dimensionality Reduction may be achieved using Feature Extraction techniques and Feature Selection procedures. Characteristic Choice selects a subset of this Original factor. Feature Extraction performs data conversion from a high dimensional space to a low dimensional space. Instance: PCA algorithm is a Feature Extraction Strategy.

## Reinforcement learning:

Reinforcement learning is a sort of machine learning algorithm which makes it possible for a broker to determine the best actions based on its current state by studying behavior that will maximize a reward.

Reinforcement algorithms learn actions that are optimum through trial and error. Imagine a game where the player should move to make points. A psychologist algorithm playing that sport could begin with moving randomly through trial and error over time, it might discover where and when had to maneuver the personality to make the most of its point overall.

# Quantifying the Popularity of Machine Learning Algorithms

Where did we get these ten calculations? Such a list will be inherently subjective. Studies like these have measured the ten most data mining algorithms; however, they are still relying on surveys to answer advanced practitioners' responses. By way of instance, from the analysis linked above, the men polled were the champions of the ACM KDD Innovation Award, the IEEE ICDM Research Contributions Award, the Program Committee members of their KDD'06, ICDM'06, and SDM'06; as well as the 145 attendees of this ICDM'06.

The top 10 algorithms are selected with machine learning beginners in mind. There are primarily calculations I learned in the 'Data Warehousing and Mining' (DWM) class within my Bachelor's degree in Computer Engineering at the University of Mumbai. I've included the previous two algorithms (outfit methods) used to acquire Kaggle competitions.

Without Further Ado Learning Algorithms for Beginners:

## 1. Linear Regression

In machine learning, we've got a group of input factors $(x)$, which are utilized to determine an outcome variable $(y)$. A connection exists between the output factor and the input variables. ML'S objective is to measure this relationship.

## Linear-Regression

In the Linear Regression Factors, the connection between the input (x) and output (y) is referred to as an equation of the type y = a + box. Therefore, the objective of linear regression is to learn the values of coefficients a and b. Here, a is the intercept and b is the slope of this line.

## 2. Logistic Regression

Linear regression prediction is constant values (i.e., Rainfall in cm); logistic regression prediction is different values (i.e., if or not a student passed/failed) after applying a transformation purpose.

Regression is best suited for binary Classification: information places were y = 1 or 0, where 1 denotes the default category. As an instance, in predicting if an event will happen or not, there are just two possibilities: that it happens (that we denote as 1) or it doesn't (0). If we predicted whether a patient was ill, we would label sick patients utilizing the value of 1 in our data set.

Logistic Regression is called after the transformation. It operates as the logistic function h(x)= 1/ (1 + ex) creating an S-shaped curve.

In logistic regression, the outcome takes the kind of probabilities of the default class (unlike linear regression, in which the output signal is directly generated). Since it's a probability, the outcome could be in the assortment of 0-1. Therefore, by way of instance, if we are attempting to predict if patients are ill, we know that ill patients have been denoted as 1, therefore if our algorithm assigns the rating of 0.98 into a patient, then it believes that individual is very likely to be sick.

This output (y-value) is made by log changing the X-value, with the logistic function h(x)= 1/ (1 + e^ -x). A threshold is employed to induce this possibility into a binary classification.

## Logistic-Function-machine-learning

The logistic regression equation P(x) = e ^ (b0 +b1x) / (1 + Portable (b0 + b1x)) could be changed to ln(p(x) / / 1-p(x)) = b0 + b1x.

Logistic regression's Objective is to utilize the training information to discover the values of coefficients b0 and b1 such that it will decrease the error between the outcome and the actual result. All these coefficients are estimated using the Maximum Likelihood Estimation method.

## 3. CART

Classification and Regression Trees (CART) are just one Execution of Decision Trees.

The no_ terminal nodes of Regression and Classification Trees would be the root node as well as the origin node. The terminal nodes are the leaf nodes. Every non-terminal node represents a single input factor (x) plus a dividing point on such factor; the leaf nodes represent the output variable (y). The design can be used as follows to create predictions: walk the breaks of this tree to arrive at the value present in the leaf node.

The decision tree in Figure 3 under classifies an individual who will purchase a minivan or a sports car based on marital status and age. If the man is over 30 decades and isn't married, into the tree walks as follows: 'over 30 decades?' ->yes -> married?' ->no. Therefore, the model outputs a sports car.

Decision-Tree-Diagram-machine-learning

## 4. Naïve Bayes

To calculate the likelihood that an event will happen, given that another event has occurred, we use Bayes's Theorem. To calculate the likelihood of theory (h) being true, given that our previous knowledge(d), we use Bayes's Theorem as follows:

$P(h|d) = (P(d|h) P(h)) / P(d)$

Where:

$P(h|d)$ = Posterior probability. The probability of hypothesis h being accurate, given the data, where $P(h|d) = P(d1| h) P(d2| h) ... P(dn| h) P(Id)$

$P(d|h)$ = Likelihood. The likelihood of data d given that the hypothesis h was authentic

$P(h)$ = Course prior probability. The probability of Hypothesis h being accurate (irrespective the data)

$P(Id)$ = Predictor prior chance. Probability of this information (no matter this hypothesis)

This algorithm is known as 'naive' since it presumes that the factors are independent of one another, and it can be a naive assumption to make in real-world cases.

## Naive-Bayes

To determine the outcome, play 'yes' or 'no' awarded the significance of varying weather =' shining,' compute P(yes|bright ), and P(no|bright ) and pick the results with greater probability.

->P(yes|bright) = (P(bright |yes) * P(yes)) / P(bright) = (3/9 * 9/14) / (5/14) = 0.60

->P(no more |bright) = (P(bright |no) * P(no)) / P(bright) = (2/5 * 5/14) / (5/14) = 0.40

If the weather_ 'shining,' the result is played_ 'yes.'

## 5. KNN

K-Nearest Neighbors algorithm uses the data set as a training set and test set rather than splitting the data set into a training set and test set.

Once an outcome is required for a data case, the algorithm goes throughout the whole data set to discover the k-nearest cases to the new case, or the number of cases most like the new document; after that outputs the expression of their results (for a regression issue ) or the mode (most common course ) for a classification issue. The value of k is user-specified.

The similarity between cases is calculated using measures like Hamming space and Euclidean space.

Unsupervised learning algorithms

# 6. Apriori

The Apriori algorithm applies in a database mine item sets then generate association rules. Market basket analysis makes large use of it. Generally, we compose the institution rule for 'when somebody buys item X, he then buys item Y' as X -> Y.

Example: when a person buys sugar and milk, then she's likely to buy coffee powder. It might be written in the kind of an association rule as undefined -> coffee powder. After crossing the threshold to get confidence and support, association rules are created.

The support step helps prune the number of candidate itemsets to be considered during item set creation. The Apriori principle guides this service step. The Apriori principle says that if an item set is regular, then all its subsets must also be regular.

# 7. K-means

K-means is an iterative algorithm that groups similar information data into clusters. It computes the centroids of k clusters and assigns a statistics to point to this audience with space between its centroid along with the information point.

Here is how it works:

We begin by picking a value of k. Here, let's state $k=3$. Then we randomly assign each data point to any of the 3 clusters. Computer cluster centroid for all one of these clusters. The red, green, and blue stars encircle the centroids for each of the three clusters.

Reassign every point to the cluster that is the nearest centroid. From the figure above, the five points obtained assigned to the audience using all the centroid. Follow the identical method to assign points to the clusters comprising the centroids that are green and red.

Compute centroids for the clusters that are new. The older centroids are gray stars; the new centroids are green, the red, and blue stars.

Repeat steps 2-3 until there's no shifting of points from one cluster to another. Once there's no shifting for two successive steps, depart the K-means algorithm.

# 8. PCA

Principal Component Analysis (PCA) can be used to create data easy to research by cutting back on the number of factors and pictures. You can achieve that by capturing the most variance in the information right into a new coordinate system with axes known as 'principal components.'

Each element is a linear combination of the first factors and can be orthogonal to one another. Orthogonality between elements suggests the correlation between these elements is zero.

The first component captures the leadership of the maximum

variability in the information. The second main component captures the residual variance from the information but has factors uncorrelated with the initial element. In the same way, all consecutive main components (PC3, PC4, and so forth) catch the rest of the variance while still being uncorrelated with the prior art.

## Learning Methods

Ensembling means combining multiple learners' results (classifiers) for enhanced outcomes by averaging or voting. Voting can be utilized during classification, and averaging is used through regression. The notion is that ensembles of students perform better than single students.

There are 3 Kinds of ensembling algorithms: Bagging, Boosting, and Stacking. We're not likely to pay 'piling' here, however, in case you'd prefer a detailed explanation of this, here is a good introduction in Kaggle.

## 9. Bagging with Random Forests

Step one into bagging is to create versions with data collections made using the Bootstrap Sampling method. In Bootstrap Sampling, every created training set is made up of the data collection of subsamples.

All these training places are of the same size; a few documents don't appear, but some documents replicate times, although original data collection. The whole data collection is the evaluation set. Therefore, if the dimensions of the initial data set are N, then the dimensions of every generated training set can also be N, together with the number of special documents being approximately (2N/3); the dimensions of this test set can also be N.

The second step in bagging is to create versions by training places that were generated by using the identical algorithm.

At this point, really where it is entered by Random Forests. Unlike for building the split decision tree, in which each node is split on the characteristic that reduces error, we pick a choice of attributes. When choice trees pick the attribute to split the main reason behind randomness is with bagging, they wind up with related predictions and similar structure.

The Amount of attributes is defined as the Random Forest algorithm as a parameter.

Therefore every tree is constructed with a sample of each record, and splits are assembled with a random sample of predictors.

## 10. Boosting with AdaBoost

Adaboost stands for Adaptive Boosting. Bagging is a parallel outfit because every model is constructed. Boosting is an outfit where every model is constructed based on adjusting their previous model's misclassifications.

Bagging involves 'voting' in which every classifier votes to acquire the last outcome one which is dependent on the vast majority of the concurrent versions. Fostering involves 'discretionary voting' where every classifier votes to acquire the last outcome that's dependent on most, but the successive models were assembled by assigning higher weights into misclassified cases of their last versions.

Of building students, the procedure continues until several learners have been assembled or till there's not any advancement while coaching. Measure 4 combines the three decision stumps of those last versions (and thus includes three dividing principles in the decision tree).

## First, begin to create a choice on a single input factor.

The dimensions of these data points show that we've applied equal weights to classify them as a triangle or a circle. The choice stump has created a line to categorize these factors. We can realize there are two circles. We employ another choice stump and will assign weights.

Move to a different choice tree stump to create a choice on a different input factor.

We see that both misclassified dimensions circles are bigger than the remaining points. Now, the choice stump will attempt to predict both of these circles.

Because of assigning weights, then both of these circles have been classified by the line on the left side. It has resulted in misclassifying the three circles on the very top. We employ another choice stump and will assign weights to those three circles.

Train yet another choice tree stump to create a choice on another input factor.

The three circles in the preceding step are bigger than the remaining data points. Now, a line to the proper is produced to classify triangles and both the circles.

Fourth, the choice that is Blend stumps.

We've combined the separators and observe the intricate rule from this version classifies data points compared to some of those students that are weak.

## Best 10 Machine Learning Algorithms for Data Science

Machine learning algorithms may seem complex and dull matter. To some degree, this is true. Typically, you stumble upon an explanation for every algorithm, and it's difficult to find energy and time to manage every detail. If you truly, madly, deeply need to be an ML-expert, then you need to brush up your understanding regarding it, and there's not anyway. But relax, now I will attempt to simplify this job and clarify the core fundamentals of 10 most frequent calculations in easy words (each includes a brief description, guides, and useful links). Breathe in, breathe out, and let us begin!

## 1. Principal Component Analysis (PCA)/SVD

That is only one of the machine learning algorithms. It allows you to lower the size of the information, losing the quantity of information; it is used in several locations, such as object recognition, computer vision, data compression, etc. The computation of these components is reduced to the singular decomposition of the data matrix or into calculating the eigenvectors and eigenvalues of the covariance matrix of the data.

Signs can be expressed by us via a single mix, so to talk, and work with a simpler model. The PCA method can enable us to minimize it, although, of course, it won't be possible to prevent information loss.

## 2a. Least Squares and Polynomial Fitting

The method of least squares is a mathematical method used to solve issues, based on reducing the number of squares of deviations of several functions from the variables. It may be used to "resolve" overdetermined systems of equations (as soon as the number of equations exceeds the number of unknowns), to look for solutions in the case of normal (not overdetermined) nonlinear systems of equations, and to approximate the point values of a specific purpose.

## 2b. Constrained Linear Regression

Least square can confuse overshoots, false areas, etc. Limits are essential to decrease the variance of this line, which we place in the information collection. The right solution would be to fit the linear regression model, which makes sure that the weights don't behave "badly."

## 3. K-Means Clustering

Clustering (or cluster analysis) is the task of dividing a pair of items into groups known as clusters. Inside each class, there ought to be "similar" items, as well as the items of distinct classes should be as distinct as you can. The difference between classification and clustering is the list of categories isn't clearly defined and can be set during this algorithm's performance.

At the same time, although the algorithm would be the easiest, inaccurate clustering method from the execution that is classical. It divides the set of components of a vector space to some previously known variety of clusters k.

The algorithm attempts to decrease the deviation at every cluster's points. The idea is that each center is recalculated for every cluster obtained in the preceding step, then vectors are broken into clusters according to which facilities were nearer in the chosen metric. The algorithm terminates when no cluster changes in any given iteration.

## 4. Logistic Regression

Logistic regression is limited to linear regression with non-linearity (sigmoid or TANH function) after employing weights; consequently, the output signal limit is near + / -- courses (which equals 0 and 1 in the case of sigmoid). Reduction functions are optimized with the gradient descent process.

Notice for logistic regression is used for classification, not regression. Generally, it's similar to a single layer neural system. Learned using optimization methods like L-BFGS or gradient descent. NLP programmers frequently use it, calling it "the maximum entropy classification process."

This is really what a sigmoid looks like.

Utilize LR to train easy, but really "powerful" classifiers.

## 5. Support Vector Machines (SVM)

SVM is a version, such as regression. The distinction is it has a reduction function. You can maximize the reduction function using optimization techniques, by way of L-BFGS instance or SGD.

## 7. Convolutional Neural Networks

Virtually all accomplishments in the field of machine dint of neural networks attained learning: object discovery, image classification, or picture segmentation use that. Networks have layers that act as thing extractors. It is possible to use them for working with text (and even for working with images).

## 8. Recurrent Neural Networks (RNNs)

Use the identical set of weights version sequences recursively into the condition of this aggregator at the time and enter at time t. Actual RNNs are seldom used today; however, its analogs, as an instance, LSTM and GRU, would be the most up-to-date in the majority of sequence modeling issues.

# 9. Conditional Random Fields (CRFs)

They're utilized to simulate a chain and may be utilized in combination with image segmentation, by way of instance, in different activities of the forecast. CRF models all arrangement elements (say a sentence), the neighbors impact the tag of this component from the arrangement rather than all tags which are independent of one another.

# 10. Decision Trees

The construction reflects the "leaves" and "branches." Characteristics of this objective function are determined by "branches" of the decision tree, the values of the objective function are the "leaves" as well as the remaining nodes comprise attributes for the instances differ.

To classify a new case, you want to go down the tree to foliage and provide the proper price. The target is to make a model that forecasts the value of this targeted factor based on input factors.

Well, if you read all the information and even click on a few guides, I congratulate you. Now's the time to bring some advice. Well, it is quite a scene when novices ask questions such as this; which algorithm to use? Might it be feasible not, and to center on a particular algorithm to look at the remainder? The reply to this sounds as follows: 'it depends on the situation.'

What does this mean? By way of example, an individual cannot states that neural networks always function. The potency of algorithms is more and influenced by several things, like construction and the dimensions of this data. Do not expect to dive in the very best algorithm; trigger it doesn't exist.

It seems unpleasant, but you must try a lot of algorithms, then pick the most suitable choice, check the potency of each on the evaluation data set. You have to pick. Here's a vivid analogy: if you have to clean your home, you may use a vacuum cleaner, a broom, or a mop; however, you would not bust out a shovel and begin digging. Be patient and don't rush things.

# CHAPTER 7

# THE BEST WAY TO USE THE SCI-KIT-LEARN LIBRARY

## What's sci-kit-learn or even learn?

Scikit-learn is most likely the library for machine learning in Python. The sklearn module library includes a whole lot of efficient instruments for machine learning and statistical modelings such as classification, regression, and clustering and dimensionality reduction.

Please be aware that learning can be used to build system learning versions. Don't use it for manipulating, studying the information, and outlining it. You will find far better libraries for this (e.g., NumPy, Pandas, etc.).

Scikit-learn Logo

Elements of sci-kit-learn:

Scikit-learn comes packed with many attributes. Listed below are a few of these to help you realize the spread:

Learning algorithms: Think about any supervised machine learning algorithm you may have heard about, and a possibility is it is a component of sci-kit-learn. Beginning from Generalized linear models (e.g., Linear Regression), Support Vector Machines (SVM),

Decision Trees to Bayesian approaches -- most of them are a part of the sci-kit-learn toolbox. The spread of machine learning algorithms is just one of the causes of the use of scikit-learn library. I began using this library to fix supervised learning issues and would recommend that to folks new to scikit / machine learning too.

Cross-validation: There is various procedures precision of models on data.

Toy datasets: This came in handy when studying sci-kit-learn. I'd heard SAS with different academic datasets (e.g., IRIS dataset, Boston House costs dataset). A whole lot was helped by having them handy while studying a brand new library.

Extraction: for pulling features of Scikit-learn from text and images (e.g., Bags of phrases)

Community / Organizations with scikit-learn:

Among the reasons behind using the open-source tools is the massive community it has. The same holds are true for sklearn as well. There are approximately 35 contributors to scikit-learn to date, the most celebrated being Andreas Mueller (P.S. Andy's machine learning sheet is among the greatest visualizations to comprehend the range of machine learning algorithms).

There are several organizations of the likes of Evernote, AWeber, and Inria that are using scikit to find the home page as a user. However, I feel that the use is much more.

There are various meetups across the world. There was a Kaggle knowledge competition, which ended but maybe among the greatest places.

**Fast Example:**

Now that you know the ecosystem at a top-level, let me exemplify sklearn's usage. The concept is to illustrate the use of learns. We'll take a look at algorithms and methods to utilize them in a few.

We'll construct a logistic regression on IRIS dataset:

Step 1: Import the libraries that are relevant and read the dataset

Import NumPy as np

Import matplotlib as plt

Out of import datasets learned

Out of import metrics learned

Out of sklearn.linear_version import Logistic Regression

All the libraries are imported. We read the dataset:

Dataset = datasets.load_iris()

Step 2: Know the dataset by taking a look at distributions and plots

These steps, for the time being, are skipping. You can read this Article if you would like to know the analysis.

Step 3: Construct a logistic regression model on the dataset and creating forecasts

```
model.fit(dataset.data, dataset.target)

ecpected = dataset.target

Predicted = model.predict(dataset.data)

Step 4: Insert confusion matrix

Publish (metrics.classification_report(expected (predicted))

Print (metrics.confusion_matrix(expected (predicted))
```

## Neural Network Definition

Neural systems are a pair of calculations, modeled following the human mind able to recognize patterns. They interpret information clustering or labeling input. The pattern they recognize is numerical in which all information that is real-world data, be it audio, pictures, text, or time collection, must be interpreted.

Systems assist us in the cluster and classify. You can believe in these as a classification and clustering coating in addition to the information you handle and store. They help based on similarities among the instance inputs, plus data is classified by them when they have a dataset. Neural networks also can extract features that fed into other algorithms such as clustering and classification; therefore, it's possible to imagine profound neural networks as elements of larger machine-learning programs involving algorithms for reinforcement learning, classification, and regression.

What type of issues does learning that is profound resolve, and much more importantly, can it solves yours? To know the answer, you have to ask questions:

What results do I care about? Those results are labels that may be applied to information within good_guy in an email address or bad_guy in fraud detection.

Can I have the information to accompany those labels? That is, can I find branded data, or can I produce a branded dataset (using a service such as AWS Mechanical Turk or Figure Eight or Mighty.ai) where spam was tagged as spam, to instruct an algorithm precisely the correlation between inputs and labels?

## A Couple of Concrete Cases

Learning maps inputs to outputs. Correlations are found by it. It's referred to as a "universal approximator," as it can learn to approximate an unknown function $f(x) = y$ involving any input and any output, presuming they're associated at all (by correlation or causation, by way of instance). From the process of studying, a neural system finds the appropriate f, or the right way of transforming x to y, whether that's $f(x) = 3x + 12$ or $f(x) = 9x - 0.1$. Listed below are a couple of examples of what learning can do?

## Classification

Datasets depends upon types of tasks; people need to transfer their knowledge to get a network to the dataset to understand the significance between information and tags. This is referred to as learning.

## Clustering

Group or clustering is the discovery of similarities. Learning doesn't need tags to discover similarities. Learning without tags is known as unsupervised learning. Information is information in the world's vast majority. One regulation of machine learning is; the more data an algorithm can train on, the more accurate it will be. Thus learning can create versions.

Detection: discovering similarities' flipside is detecting behavior that is odd or anomalies. Frequently, strange behavior correlates highly with matters that you wish to detect and stop, for example, fraud.

## Predictive Analytics: Regressions

With classification, learning can establish correlations between, say, the title of somebody and pixels within a picture. You may call this kind of forecast that is static. By the identical token, exposed to a lot of the data learning can establish correlations between events and future events. It may run regression between the near future and the past. The upcoming occasion that is similar to the tag in ways. Learning does take care of even the simple fact, or time that something has not occurred yet. Given a period of learning, forecast the amount likely to happen and can read a series of numbers.

## Worker turnover (ditto, but for workers)

The better we could forecast, the better we can stop and pre-empt. We are moving towards a world of surprises, as you can see, together with networks. Not zero surprises. We are moving toward a world of agents that combine neural networks with algorithms.

With this summary of learning usage cases that are profound, let us look at what exactly nets are made from.

## Neural Network Elements

Deep learning is the title we use for "piled neural Networks"; this is, networks made up of numerous layers.

## Curious in reinforcement learning?

The layers are built from nodes. A node is a location where computation occurs stitched to a neuron as it experiences stimulation that is sufficient in mind, which fires. A node joins input in the data using a pair of coefficients, or weights, so which either amplify or dampen that enter signal, thereby assigning importance to inputs concerning the activity the algorithm is attempting to find out; e.g., which input is the most useful is classifying information without error? These goods are summed, and the amount is passed via the so-called stimulation feature of a node to ascertain to what extent, which indicates should advance further to impact the result and whether state, an act of classification. If the signal passes through, the neuron was "triggered.

Following is a diagram of exactly what one node may look like.

## Perceptron node

A coating that is node is a row of these neuron-like switches that the input signal is fed via the internet, turn off, or on. The output of every layer signal is the input signal, beginning from an initial layer receiving your data.

## Multilayer perceptron

Pairing the flexible weights of the model using input attributes is we assign value to the network clusters and classifies input.

## Key Concepts of Deep Neural Networks

Networks are different from more commonplace networks because of their thickness; this is, the number of layers by which data must pass in a multistep process of pattern recognition.

Versions like the first of networks Perceptions were shallow, composed of one input and one output, and at the most a hidden layer in between. Over three layers (like output and input) qualify as "deep" learning. So profound isn't merely a buzzword listening and to earn calculations look as they read Sartre. It is a defined term, which means more than just one layer.

In deep-learning networks, each layer of nodes trains a set of attributes depending on the output of the layer. The further the attributes, your nodes may recognize progress into the net, recombine, and because they aggregate attributes from the last layer.

152

## Attribute hierarchy

It is a hierarchy of increasing abstraction and sophistication. It creates networks capable of managing big data collections with billions of parameters.

Most importantly, these nets are effective at detecting latent structures within the information, which is the majority of information on earth. Another term for unstructured information is raw websites, i.e., images, texts, audio, and video records. Hence, among the issues, deep learning surpasses greatest is in communicating and clustering the planet's raw, unlabeled networking, differentiating similarities and anomalies in data that nobody has arranged into a relational database or put a name into.

By way of example, a thousand pictures can be taken by profound learning cluster them based on their similarities: cats at each of the pictures of your grandma, and one corner, ice cubes in a different. This is the cornerstone of photograph albums.

Now apply that idea deep could cluster text such as information posts or emails. While clients, or messages, may cluster others emails full of complaints can cluster in 1 corner of the vector area. This is the cornerstone of different messaging filters, also may be utilized in customer-relationship management (CRM). The same applies to voice messages.

Info could cluster around behavior and anomalous/dangerous behavior. In case the time series data has been generated by a wise phone, it is going to offer insight into customers' health and customs; if it's being generated by an auto part, then it may be utilized to stop catastrophic breakdowns.

Systems perform feature extraction without intervention algorithms. Given that attribute, extraction is a job that may take teams of information scientists to achieve learning is a means to bypass the chokepoint of specialists that are restricted. It reinforces the powers.

When the instruction on data, each node coating in a profound Network learns attributes automatically by repeatedly attempting to rebuild the input in which it brings its samples, trying to lessen the gap between the network guesses and also the likelihood distribution of the input itself. Restricted Boltzmann machines, for cases, make reconstructions in this way.

In the procedure, these networks learn how to recognize correlations between particular relevant features and optimum results -- they draw links between attribute signals and exactly what these attributes signify if it is a complete reconstruction, or using tagged data.

A system may be applied, providing it access to input than nets that were machine-learning. It can be a recipe for functionality: the more information web can train, the more precise it is very likely to be. (Bad algorithms educated on plenty of info can outperform fantastic algorithms trained on hardly very little). It is given a

154

distinct advantage over previous calculations by learning's capacity to process and learn out of amounts of data.

Networks wind within an output: a logistic, or softmax, a classifier that assigns a chance to tag or a specific result. It's predictive in a sense, although we call that predictive. A deep-learning network with raw information in the shape of a picture can decide, by way of instance, that the input information is 90 percent likely to be a symbol of an individual.

## Instance: Feedforward Networks

With a neural net, our goal would be to arrive at the stage of least error as possible. We're conducting a race, along with the race, is about a course, so we pass the very same points repeatedly in a loop. The starting lineup for the race would be that the condition where our weights are initialized and the end line is the condition of these parameters when they're capable of generating sufficiently precise predictions and groups.

The race those steps, and each resembles the measures afterward and before. Just an act will participate in the above and over to reach the end. Each measure to get a neural network entails a guess, a mistake dimension plus a slight upgrade in its weights, an incremental adjustment to the coefficients, as it gradually learns to focus on the main capabilities.

An assortment of weights, whether they are in their beginning or end condition, can also be referred to as a model, since it's an effort to simulate data's connection to ground-truth labels, to grasp the information's structure. Models normally begin bad and end up less poor, changing over time since the neural network upgrades its parameters.

It can be because there is a system created in ignorance. It doesn't understand which biases and weights will interpret the input to create the guesses. It must begin using a suspect, and then try to make better guesses as it learns from its mistakes. (You may think about a neural system as a tiny enactment of this scientific procedure, testing hypotheses and attempting again -- only it's the scientific system with a blindfold on. Or just like a kid: they're born not understanding, and during exposure to lifetime experience, they learn how to fix problems. For neural networks, information is the sole encounter)

Here's a simple explanation of what happens during studying using a feed-forward network, the easiest architecture to describe.

Input enters the system. Weights, or the coefficients, map that input into some guesses the system makes at the end.

## Input* weight_ guess

Input ends in a suspect about what that input is. The neural system then takes its figure and contrasts it to some ground-truth concerning the information, effectively requesting an expert, "Did I get this right?"

Ground reality - guess = mistake

The gap between the guess and the floor of the network truth is its mistake. The system walks the mistake back over its model and measures that mistake.

Mistake * the donation to malfunction or error_adjustment

These are three formulas for your above account about three purposes of systems: calculating reduction signal, scoring input, and implementing an upgrade to the design, to start over the procedure again. A network is rewarding weights that encourage its guesses, a feedback loop, and weights, which cause it to err.

## Multiple Linear Regression

Inspired artificial neural, title networks are not anything more than code and mathematics. In reality, one of the approaches you learn in data, anybody who knows regression, can comprehend the way the neural net functions. In its most straightforward form, linear regression shows itself as:

Y_hat_ bX + a

X is the input b is the slope, the input signal where Y_hat is your output A, and the incline is the intercept of a line onto the axis of a graph that is a two-dimensional graph. (To make this concrete: X might be radiation exposure, and Y might be the cancer threat; X might be a daily routine, and Y_hat might be the entire weight which you may benchpress; X the quantity of fertilizer and Y_hat how big this harvest.) It's possible to imagine that each time you add X, then the factor Y_hat increases and a device, however far you're about the X-axis. That relation between two factors moving down or up is a beginning point.

The next step is to envision multiple regressions, where you have input factors. It is usually written like this:

Y_hat X_1 + b_2*X_2 + b_3*X_3 + a

(To expand the crop example above, you may add the amount Of sun and rain in a growing period into the fertilizer factor, together with all three affecting Y_hat.)

That kind of multiple regressions is currently occurring at each node of a system. For every node of one coating, input from every node of the coating is recombined with the input of every other node. In other words, the inputs are blended based on their coefficients, which can be different, contributing to every node of the layer. This manner, web tests in which a blend of input is important since it attempts to decrease error.

It is as soon as you sum your inputs to arrive in y_hat passed via a function. Here is the reason: if each node did multiple linear regressions, y_hat would increase with no limitation as to the growth of the X and linearly, but it does not suit our purposes.

What we're attempting to construct at each node is a switch (such as a neuron) that works off and on, based on whether it should allow the sign of the input through to impact the ultimate conclusions of this system.

You own a classification issue, whenever you've got a chance. Is it true that the signal of the input implies it should be classified by the node not_enough, or enough, away or on? A binary choice can be voiced by 0 and 1, and logistic regression is a non-linear role that squashes input signal to interpret into a distance between 1 and 0.

The nonlinear transforms at each node are functions, much like logistic regression. They go by the titles of the sigmoid (the Greek term for "S"), tanh, challenging tanh, etc., plus they forming the output of every node. The output of nodes, every squashed to an s-shaped distance between 1 and 0, is subsequently passed as input into another layer at a feed-forward neural network, etc. until the signal reaches the last layer of the internet, where choices are made.

## Gradient Descent

The title for one used optimization function that adjusts weights based on the mistake they caused is known as "gradient descent."

The gradient is just another word for slope, and incline, in its normal type within an x-y chart, reflects how two factors relate to each other: grow above run, the shift in the currency over the shift in time, etc. In this specific scenario, the incline we care about explains the association between the system's mistake and just one weight, i.e., that is, just how the mistake can vary as the burden is corrected.

To put on it, which burden will create the least mistake? The signs in the input information, and translates them are properly represented by which classification? Which you can hear "nose" in an input image, and be aware that ought to be tagged as a face rather than a skillet?

Weights are gradually adjusted by it, as a network learns, so to significance 9, they can sign. The association between networks error those weights, and each is a derivative, dE/DW, which measures the level to which a shift in a weight reduction causes a shift from the error.

Each weight is just one variable in a network that is profound which entails many changes; the sign of the weight moves through activations and amounts over many layers. Therefore we use the chain rule of calculus to march back through the activations and sparks of the network and ultimately arrive in the weight in question and its connection to general error.

## The chain rule in calculus says that

Chain rule

The connection between the internet's Mistake and one weight will look something like that:

## Backdrop series rule

Given a weight, error, and two factors, which are depending on a third factor, activation, once the weight is passed, you can compute just how a change in fat changes and alteration in error. Calculating a change in stimulation affects an alteration in feeling, and the way the change in weight influences a change inactivation.

The heart of learning in DL is nothing more than this: adjusting the weight in the reaction of a model to this error it generates, till you can't reduce the error.

## Optimization Algorithms

A few examples of optimization algorithms comprise:

- ADADELTA
- ADAGRAD
- ADAM
- NESTEROVS
- NONE
- RMSPROP
- SGD
- CONJUGATE GRADIENT
- HESSIAN FREE
- LBFGS
- LINE GRADIENT DESCENT
- Activation Functions

The output that a node will generate is determined by the activation function, based upon its input.

Some examples include:

- CUBE
- ELU
- HARDSIGMOID
- HARDTANH
- IDENTITY
- LEAKYRELU
- RATIONALTANH
- RELU
- RRELU
- SIGMOID
- SOFTMAX
- SOFT PLUS
- SOFT SIGN
- TANH

## Logistic Regression

On a profound network of layers, the coating has a function. When coping with input that is tagged signal, the output classifies each instance, employing the most likely tag. One tag is represented by every node on the output layer, which node turns off or on based on the strength of this signal it receives in parameters and the layer's input.

Each output node generates the binary, two possible results output values 1 or 0, as an input factor that warrants a tag, or it doesn't. There is absolutely no such thing as a tiny pregnant.

While networks functioning with data that is tagged create the input they get signal, the output is constant. In other words, the signs that the system receives as input contain any variety of metrics and signal will span a variety of values, based upon the problem it attempts to fix.

By way of example, a recommendation engine must make a binary choice about whether to serve an advertisement or not. However, the input it bases its choice could include how frequently the website is visited by that client, or just how much a client has spent in the previous week on Amazon.

Hence that the output has to condense signals, for example, $67.59 spent leftovers, and 15 visits to some site, right into a range between 1 and 0; i.e., a likelihood that a given input ought to be tagged or not.

The mechanism we use to convert signals that are constant into output signal is known as regression. Because regression is used for classification instead of regression, which individuals are knowledgeable about, the title is unfortunate. It computes the likelihood that the tag is matched by a pair of inputs.

## Logistic regression

For inputs to be expressed as probabilities as there's absolutely no such thing as a possibility must output benefits. That is why you see enter since the exponent of e since exponents induce our outcomes to be higher. Think about the connection between e's exponents. Certainly, as we all know, is the ceiling of a chance, beyond which our results can't go without being absurd. (We are 120% convinced of this.)

Since the input x which triggers there develops a tag, the term e Into the x shrinks toward zero, leaving us with the percent 1/1, or 100 percent, so we approach (without ever really reaching) absolute certainty which the tag applies. Input that correlates negatively with your output signal will have its worth flipped from the negative signal on e's exponent, and because negative sign develops, the amount e to the x gets bigger, pushing the whole percentage ever nearer to zero.

Imagine that, instead of having x as the exponent, you have the amount of the goods of their inputs along with weights plus corresponding input -- that the signal passes through your network. That is what you are feeding in the output of a neural network classifier to the regression coating.

With this coating, we could set a decision threshold over which a good instance is labeled as 1, and under which it isn't. You can set thresholds as you would like -- a greater one will raise the number of false negatives -- depending on which side you'd love to err, and a threshold increases the number of false positives.

## Neural Networks & Artificial Intelligence

In certain circles, neural networks are considered as "brute Induce" AI, since they begin with a blank slate and then shake their way through into a precise version. They are powerful but to some eye, inefficient in their approach to modeling, which cannot make assumptions about dependencies between input and output.

Nevertheless, every weight is not being recombined by gradient descent to discover the game; its method of pathfinding shrinks the amount of computation and updates, and so the weight area, by orders of magnitude. Algorithms like the capsule networks of Hinton demand cases of information to converge on an accurate version; that is, research that currently can solve the force character of learning that is profound.

## Described: Neural networks

Learning is a name for a way to neural networks, which have been moving in and out of vogue for at least 70 decades were known as by intelligence. Networks were suggested in 1944 from Warren McCullough and Walter Pitts, two University of Chicago investigators who transferred to MIT as profound members of what is sometimes known as the science division in 1952.

The method dropped into eclipse from this century's first decade and has returned just like gangbusters at the moment, fueled by the processing power of chips.

"There is this notion that ideas in science are somewhat like epidemics of viruses," states Tomaso Poggio, the Eugene McDermott Professor of Brain and Cognitive Sciences at MIT, a researcher at MIT's McGovern Institute for Brain Research, and director of MIT's Center for Brains, Minds, and Machines. "There are five or six primary strains of influenza viruses, and seemingly each one comes with a span of around 25 decades. People today become infected, and they create an immune reaction, and thus they do not get infected for another 25 decades. And there is a new generation that is ready to be infected by the same strain of the virus. Folks fall in love, get excited about it, get immunized, and then hammer it to death. So thoughts should have exactly the identical sort of periodicity!"

## Weighty things

Neural nets are a way of performing machine by assessing training examples; a computer learns how to execute some activity. The cases are hand-labeled beforehand. An object recognition system, for example, could be fed so on and tens of thousands of pictures of automobiles, homes, coffee cups, also it would discover patterns.

A neural net includes thousands or millions of processing nodes that are interconnected as modeled in mind. Nearly all of the current neural nets are arranged into layers of nodes, plus they are "feed-forward," meaning that information moves in just one direction. A single node may be attached to nodes in the layer to which it transmits information, where it receives information and nodes at the layer above it.

To its entire links that are incoming, a node will assign an amount called a "weight" After the system is busy, the node receives a data item -- a number that is different – over each of its connections and multiplies it by the associated weight. It then adds the products producing a single amount. If this amount is below a threshold value, no information is passed from the node. If the amount exceeds the threshold value, the node "fires," that in the neural nets generally means sending the amount -- the amount of the inputs -- together all of its incoming connections.

When there is a net being trained, its weights and all thresholds are set to random values. Training information is fed into the base layer (input layer), and it moves through the layers until it arrives, becoming multiplied and added together in complicated ways. The weights and thresholds are adjusted until training information using the labels yield outputs.

## Minds and machines

The nets clarified by Pitts and McCullough at 1944'd weights and thresholds; however, they were not organized to layers, and the investigators did not define any coaching mechanism. What Pitts and McCullough demonstrated was that a neural net could, in principle, calculate any function which a computer could. The result was neuroscience than computer science: the purpose was to imply the human mind may be considered as a device.

Nets are still being a valuable instrument for neuroscientific research. For example, for correcting weights and thresholds have replicated rules or specific network layouts observed characteristics of cognition and neuroanatomy, a sign that they catch something about the way information is processed by the brain.

The perceptron, the very first neural system, was demonstrated in 1957 from the Cornell University psychologist Frank Rosenblatt. The Perceptron's layout was similar to the contemporary net, except that it had just one layer sandwiched between input and output layers, with weights and thresholds.

Perceptions have been an active area of study in both Psychologies as well as the fledgling field of computer science before 1959 when Minsky and Papert released a book titled "Perceptrons," which revealed that implementing certain quite common computations on perceptrons are impractically time-consuming.

"All these constraints kind of evaporate if you make machines that are a bit more complex -- such as, just two layers," Poggio states. But at the moment, the publication had a chilling impact on research that is neural-net.

"You've got to place these items in historical context," Poggio says." They were contending for programming -- for languages such as Lisp. Not a Lot People still used computers. It wasn't clear in any way that programming has been the best way to go. I think they moved a bit as usual, although overboard, it is not white and black. Should you think of them as this Rivalry involving computing that was analog and computing struggled for what in the time was the ideal thing?"

## Periodicity

From the 1980s, however, calculations had been developed by researchers for modifying nets' weights and thresholds, which were effective enough eliminating lots of the constraints identified by Minsky and Papert. The area enjoyed a renaissance.

But there is something neural nets. Training can revise the settings of a network to the stage; it may categorize information, but what exactly do these settings mean? Is a thing recognizer considering, and how can this slice them together to automobiles, homes, and coffee cups' visual signatures? By taking a look at the weights of relations, that query won't be answered.

Lately, computer scientists have begun to develop procedures for deducing the strategies adopted by nets. But from the 1980s, the networks' plans were indecipherable. So round the turn of the century, support vector machines, and way of machine learning that is based on some refined and very tidy mathematics supplanted neural networks.

The resurgence in neural networks -- that the deep-learning Revolution -- comes courtesy of this industry. The intricate imagery and rapid speed of the video games need hardware that could sustain, and the consequence is the graphics processing unit (GPU), which packs tens of thousands of relatively easy processing cores on a single processor. It did not take long to understand that a GPU's structure is remarkably similar to that of a net.

Modern GPUs allowed the networks of the 1960s and both - to - three-layer networks of the 1980s to blossom to the 10-, 15-, even networks of today, what the "deep" in "deep learning" describes, that is the thickness of their system's layers. And now, learning is accountable for the systems in every subject of research.

## Below the hood

The networks' opacity is unsettling to theorists; there is headway on that front. In addition to directing the Center for Brains, Minds, and Machines (CBMM), Poggio directs the center's research program in Theoretical Frameworks for Intelligence. Lately, Poggio and his colleagues that were CBMM, have published a study of networks.

The first part that was published last month at the International Journal of Computing and Automation addresses the variety of computations if networks provide benefits over ones and which networks may execute. Components two and three that have been published as CBMM technical reports tackle the issues of digital marketing, or even reassuring that a community has discovered the settings that best accord with its training information, and overfitting; there are even instances where the system gets so conducive to the particulars of its training information it fails to generalize to other cases of the same categories.

There are lots of concerns that are theoretical to be replied, but CBMM investigators' work might help make sure that the cycle which has brought them in and out in favor for seven years is eventually broken by networks.

www.ingramcontent.com/pod-product-compliance
Lightning Source LLC
Chambersburg PA
CBHW071248050326
40690CB00011B/2302